Anglotopia's Dictionary of British English

British Slang from A to Zed

Jonathan Thomas

Anglotopia

ALSO BY ANGLOTOPIA

To my lovely wife, Jackie

Table of Contents

Introduction

We've all been there. We're watching a charming British TV show and enjoying all it has to offer and then suddenly you hear a word used in a strange way and you don't understand the meaning.

While Americans and the British speak the same language, the British use many words differently than we do. So, we thought it would be fun to write a dictionary to British English - geared towards viewers of British TV.

No longer will you have to scratch your head about the meaning of something. With this dictionary by your side, you'll always have a way to translate from Brit speak to American English.

It was not possible to include every word the British use differently without it becoming an actual dictionary so we've limited the list to more common words and phrases. Most of our definitions are based on comparisons to American English so that's the perspective from which we have written.

We've excluded words that basically have the same meaning in both American and British English and there are a lot of words that were cut because there is no need to be redundant, we wanted this text to be a quick reference.

Other British Slang Dictionaries separate words by category, we dispensed with that and made one master dictionary of all British English words and created several sections exploring distinct dialects of British English (such as Scouse, Yorkshire, West Country, etc).

A bit of warning, we have included everyday words as well as offensive and derogatory terms. This is for educational purposes and we certainly don't advocate insulting people. But it would be nice to be armed with the knowledge of what a particular insult means.

If you feel we've forgotten a word, there is a handy form in the back of the book that you can cut out send it to us so we can consider it for inclusion in the next edition.

Enjoy!

Cheers,
Jonathan
Anglophile-in-Chief
Anglotopia

A

AA - *abbr* - The British Automobile Association, whom you call when your car breaks down.

A&E - *n* - Accident and Emergency, what Americans would call the Emergency Room.

A - Levels - *n* - The highest level of secondary education that culminates in a series of standardized tests.

Abattoir - *n* - A place where an animal is butchered.

Abdabs - *n* - To be scared or frightened of something.

Absobloodylootely - *n* - To agree with someone highly in a rather enthusiastic fashion. Somewhat vulgar.

Ace - *n* - Excellent or wonderful.

Action man - *n* - The equivalent to the U.S. G.I. Joe or a man that does macho things.

Advert - *n* - An advertisement or commercial.

Aerial - *n* - A television antenna, usually located on the roof.

Aeroplane - *n* - How the British spell 'airplane'.

Afters - *n* - Another name for the dessert course at dinner.

AGA - *n* - A massive cooking range modeled with a vintage look.

Aggro - *n* - Abbreviation of "aggravation". Something that is rather annoying.

Agony Aunt - *n* - A newspaper advice columnist.

Air Biscuit - *n* - A fart.

Airy-Fairy - *adj* - Someone who is lacking in strength or ability.

Alcopop - *n* - Canned or carbonated fruit drinks with alcohol in them.

Aled up - *adj* - To be drunk as the result of drinking ale.

Alight - *v* - To disembark or get off a mode of transport like a train or bus.

All fur coat and no knickers - *adj* - A woman who looks good on the surface but has no substance.

All Mod Cons - *n* - A home or car with all the modern conveniences.

All mouth and no trousers - *adj* - To be boastful without justification.

All over the Gaff - *n* - To be disorganized.

All over the shop - *adj* - **1.** To be disorganized. **2.** Everywhere

All to pot - *adj* - Something that's gone completely wrong.

Allotment - *n* - A garden plot in a shared community garden.

Alright! - *exlam* - A simple greeting. It's not a question asking how you are.

Aluminium - *n* - It's just Aluminum.

Amber nectar - *n* - Lager (beer).

Anchors - *n* - Brakes on a car.

Ankle-biters - *adj* - A derogatory term for children.

Anorak - *n* - **1.** A nerd or someone who is geeky about something like a planespotter, trainspotter or Anglophile. **2.** A light waterproof jacket perfect for rambling in the countryside.

Answerphone - *n* - An answering machine. Bit of an outdated term now that voicemail is common.

Anti-clockwise - *adv* - It means the same thing as 'counter clockwise.'

Antenatal - *adj* - Prenatal care.

Argue the toss - *v* - To dispute something at length.

Argy-bargy - *n* - Trouble, noisy or having an argument.

Arrows - *n* - Another word for darts, the actual darts themselves, not the game.

Arse - *n* - Buttocks.

Arse about Face - Back to front.

Arsehole - *n* - An asshole.

Arsemonger - *n* - A person worthy of contempt.

Arse-over-tit - *adj* - To fall over, often as the result of alcohol. To be intoxicated.

As rare as hen's teeth - *adj* - Something that's rare.

ASBO - *n* - Anti-social behavior order - a punishment on people who repeatedly disturb the peace.

Aubergine - *n* - Otherwise known as an eggplant.

Aussie kiss - *n* - Oral sex on a woman.

Autumn - *n* - The British don't have Fall, they have Autumn, the season that precedes winter.

Axe - *n* - A guitar.

Axe wound - *n* - Vagina.

B

Baby batter - *n* - Semen.
Backhander - *n* - Bribe.
Back passage - *n* - Anus.
Back scuttle - *n* - Anal intercourse.
Badger - *v* - To annoy someone incessantly.
Bagsie - *v* - Calling dibbs on something. For example, I call bagsies on the front seat of the car.
Bairn - *n* - Another word for baby, usually used in Scotland.
Baldy notion - *n* - To have an idea or a clue about something.
Ball bag - *n* - Scrotum.
Balloon Knot - *n*- The anus.
Ballsed up - *adj* - A situation that's all messed up.
Bally - *n* - Short for Balaclava, a type of mask that covers your face.
Bare - *n* - To say that there is a lot of something.

Baltic - *n* - To describe something as very cold, referring to the Baltic region.
Banger - *n* - Short term for the traditional English sausage. When served with mashed potatoes, it's called bangers and mash.
Bang on - *adj* - Exactly or correct.
Bang out of order - *adj* - Totally unacceptable.
Bank Holiday - *n* - A public holiday in the UK. Usually they don't have any special meaning other than a day off that allows a long weekend. However, Christmas, Boxing Day etc are usually Bank Holidays as well.
Bap - *n* - A breadroll.
Baps - *n* - Another name for a woman's breasts.
Barking - *adj* - Insane or crazy.

Barmpot - *n* - A stupid person that has the added distinction of being clumsy.

Barmy - *adj* - To be crazy or insane.

Barnet - *n* - Another name for human hair, Cockney roots in the location of Barnet.

Barney - *n* - To be in big trouble.

Barrister - *n* - A lawyer that practices in front of higher court judges.

Bash on - *interj* - To go on regardless of the problems facing you in a situation.

Bean - *n* - 1. An ecstasy pill 2. The female clitoris.

Bearded clam - *n* - Female genetalia that's covered in pubic hair.

Beat the bishop - *v* - To masturbate.

Beavering - *v* - To work industriously at something. Not used as much these days because of what the word 'beaver' means in American English.

Bee's Knees, The - *adj* - Something that is awesome and wonderful.

Bedfordshire - *n* - Bed or bedtime. Said as "I'm off to Bedfordshire."

Bedsit - *n* - An apartment where the bedroom serves as the living space similar to a studio apartment.

Beeb - *n* - Shorthand for the BBC.

Belisha Beacons - *n* - The yellow flashing lights at a pedestrian crossing in the UK.

Bell-end - *n* - The end of the male genetalia. Also an insult to call someone stupid. "Don't be such a bell-end."

Belt Up - *interj* - Shut up.

Bender - *n* - 1. An epic alcohol drinking session. 2. A derogatory term for a male homosexual.

Bent - *n* - A derogatory term for a homosexual.

Berk - *n* - An idiot or irritating person.

Bespoke - *adj* - Something that is custom made for you. i.e. bespoke cabinetry.

Best of British - *v* - To wish someone good luck.

Bevvy - *n* - An Alcoholic drink.

Bill, The - *n* - A slang term for the Police.

Billy no-mates - *n* - A person who doesn't have any friends.

Billy - *n* - Amphetamine drugs.

Bin - *n* - A trashcan.

Bin liner - *n* - A garbage bag that goes in a trashcan.

Bin man - *n* - Garbage man.

Bint - *n* - A derogatory word for woman who is just above a prostitute.

Bird - *pron* - An attractive girl or woman.

Biro - *n* - A ball point pen.

Biscuit - n - What Americans call a cookie. As a corollary it has nothing to do with what Americans call a biscuit.

Bits and bobs - *n* - Bits and pieces.

Blag - *v* - To scam something. Blagging is to pretend to be someone else to steal their personal information or access their bank accounts.

Bleeding - *adj* - Another use of the word bloody.

Blighter - *adj* - A man or a boy.

Blighty - *n* - An older term that simply means Britain.

Blimey - *interj* - Exclamation similar to "Oh no!" or "Oh dear!"

Blinding - *adj* - Something that is uniquely wonderful

Blink - *adj* - Something that's not working. "On the blink."

Blinking - *adj* - Damned.

Bloke - *n* - Guy or man.

Bloody - *adj* - The British equivalent to the word damn and it is considered a mild curse word.

Blooming - *adj* - A much lighter way to say bloody. The American equivalent would be 'darn.'

Blow off - *v* - Fart.

Blower - *n* - Telephone.

Blub - *v* - To cry.

Bob - *n* - 5 pence piece (used to be a shilling)

Bob's your uncle - *interj* - There you have it!

Bobbie - *n* - Police officer.

Bobbins - *adj* - Something that's crap.

Bodge - *v* - Something haphazard or cobbled together.

Bodge job - *n* - A poorly done job.

Bodger - *n* - A person who works with wood, a wood turner.

Boff - *v* - To have sexual intercourse.

Boffin - *n* - Policy wonk or someone that is knowledgeable on a subject.

Bog - *n* - The toilet.

Bog roll - *n* - Toilet paper.

Bog standard - *n* - Normal or average.

Bogie - *n pron* - A booger.

Boiler - *n* - An unkind term for an ugly woman.

Bollard - *n* - Metal post that usually indicates a place one should not drive into.

Bollocks - *n* - 1. Male testicles. 2. Something that is rubbish or crap.

Bollocking - *n* - To be punished severely or told off.

Bolshie - *adj* - A rebel.

Bolt-hole - *n* - A hideaway place, usually a country cottage.

Bomb - *n* - A splendid success.

Bonce - *n* - The top of one's head.

Bonfire night - *n* - Also known as Guy Fawkes Day, fireworks and bonfires are usually held to celebrate the capture of Guy Fawkes.

Bonnet - *n* - The hood of a car.

Bonny - *adj* - Scottish for beautiful.

Boot - *n* - The car's trunk, opposite of the bonnet.

Boozer - *n* - A pub or bar.

Boracic - *n* - Without money. From rhyming slang 'Boracic Lint' - Skint.

Bottle - *n* - To have a lot of nerve. He's got a lot of bottle!

Bounder - *n* - A useless person.

Box - n - A rather rude way to refer to the female genitalia.

Boxing Day - *n* - The day after Christmas. A public holiday where everyone has the day off but doesn't really have any special meaning anymore.

Braces - *n* - Suspenders.

Brackets - *n* - Parentheses. '( )'

Brassed Off - *adj* - To be fed up with something that's frustrating you. Similar to 'pissed off' in American English.

Break wind - *v* - Fart.

Brekky - *n* - Breakfast.

Brew - *n* - A cup of tea.

Brick - *n* - A person that you can rely on.

Bricking it - *n* - Someone who is terrified.

Brill - *adj* - Short for brilliant!

Brilliant! - *adj* - Exclamation for something that is awesome.

Brolly - *n* - Umbrella.

Brownfield land - *n* - Former industrial land that is available for re-use.

Brush - *n* - A broom.

BSE - Acronym - Mad Cow Disease.

Bubble and squeak - *n* - Boiled cabbage and sausage.

Buff - *adj* - Sexually attractive; Also a word for nude, sometimes used loosely to describe the act of sex e.g. "We was buffin' for hours."

Bugger - *n* - An exclamation of dissatisfaction ("Oh bugger!"), in a dire situation ("Well, we're buggered now"), acute surprise ("Well bugger me!"), dismissal ("bugger that").

Buggery - *n* - The act of anal sex.

Builder - *n* - A construction worker or contractor.

Builder's bum - *adj* - Plumber's crack.

Builder's tea - *n* - Strong, inexpensive tea taken by people in the building trade, usually in a mug.

Bum - *n, v* - Buttocks. Not particularly rude - more acceptable in polite circles than 'arse.'

Bum bag - *n*- What Americans would call a fanny pack (don't call it a fanny pack in the UK, see 'fanny'.)

Bum bandit - *n* - Homosexual, derogatory.

Bum cleavage - *n* - The area between the buttocks.

Bumf - *n* - Too much paperwork.

Bung - *n* - To give or throw a game.

Bunk off - *v* - To call off sick or not fulfil your duties.

Burgle - *n* - To break into a building.

Busker - *v* - Street musician.

Butcher's - *n* - To look at something.

Butty - *n* - A sandwich usually sold in chip shops that consists of sausages and chips. Or both.

Brew - *n* - A cup of tea.

C

C of E - *n* - A short way of saying Church of England - England's official state Church.

Cabbage - *n* - 1. Vegetable 2. Someone who is brain-dead or catatonic.

Cack - *n* - Shit.

Cack-handed - *n* - Clumsy or inept.

Caff - *n* - A café.

Cakehole - *n* - Mouth - 'shut your cakehole'

Camp - *adj* - Effeminate or homosexual.

Camper van - *n* - Recreational vehicle.

Candy floss - *n* - Cotton Candy.

Cans - *n* - Headphones.

Car boot sale - *n* - Swap meet or flea market where people sell items from the back of their car.

Car park - *n* - Parking lot or parking garage.

Caravan - *n* - Another term for Recreational Vehicle.

Cardie - *n* - Short for cardigan which is a type of sweater.

Carrier bag - *n* - Shopping bag.

Carry on - *v* - To continue with something.

Cat's eyes - *n* - Reflectors located on the road in the center line.

Central reservation - *n* - The median of the road.

Chancer - *n* - A person willing to take risks or take a chance.

Chap - *n* - A man, bloke or guy.

Chat up - *v* - Trying to pick someone up in a bar or elsewhere.

Chattering Classes - *n* - Snobby upper class people chiming in on something.

Chav - *n* - A derogatory term used towards the lower classes with a similar meaning to 'white trash' but applies to all races.

Chavtastic - *n* - Something that is in poor taste that a Chav would appreciate.

Cheeky - *adj* - Risqué or too clever.

Cheerio - *interj* - Goodbye!

Cheers - *interj* - Simply means thank you but it also works as a drinking toast.

Chelp - *v* - To disagree vocally with someone without sufficient grounds to do so.

Chemist - *n* - Pharmacist but it should be noted they can also provide simple medical advice without having to go to a doctor.

Chesterfield - *n* - Hard leather sofa.

Chinese Whispers - *n* - What Americans would call Chinese Telephone.

Chipolata - *n* - A small sausage.

Chippy - *n* - A fish and chip shop.

Chips - *n* - French Fries, usually thick cut.

Chivvy on - *v* - To hurry along.

Chock-a-block - *adj* - Closely packed together i.e. a busy schedule.

Chocolate box - *adj* - Excessively decorative and sentimental, like the old pictures on boxes of candy. Usually used to describe a quaint village.

Chocolate drops - *n* - Chocolate chips.

Christmas Cracker - *n* - A Christmas tradition in England. It's a tube, nicely wrapped with a small explosive inside so when you open it there's a loud pop. Inside is a token prize, a joke and a paper crown. Usually done at Christmas Dinner.

Chinless Wonder - *adj* - A person of upper class extraction who's clueless or lacks depth of character.

Chuff - *v* - Fart.

Chuffed - *adj* - To be quite pleased about something, not to be confused with the singular version above.

Chugger - *n* - Short for charity mugger, someone who prowls Britain's high streets and pressures people to donate money to charities (they earn a commission on each donation).

Chunder - *v* - To vomit.

Chunky Chips - n - Very thick cut French fries.

Cider - *n* - Alcoholic form of apple juice.

Ciggy - *n* - A cigarette.

Clone town - *n* - The process where all the high streets in Britain have the same big chain stores so they all look pretty much the same and push out small local businesses.

Close - *n* - A cul-de-sac.

Clunge - *n* - A very very rude word for the female vagina not to be used in polite or even impolite conversation.

Coach - *n* - A bus.

Cobblers - *n* - Stupid nonsense. Similar to rubbish.

Cock - *adj* - A very versatile insult but basically an idiot.

Cock-up - *v* - To mess something up really badly.

Codswallop - *n* - Nonsense.

Colleague - *n* - Co-worker

College - *n* - A school that specializes in single year studies. Done between leaving school and going to a university.

Collywobbles - *n* - The heebie-jeebies.

Come a Cropper - *v* - To fail miserably.

Concession - *n* - A discount for a specific group (seniors, students, etc).

Confuddled - *v* - To be confused or not understand a situation.

Cooker - *n* - Otherwise known as an oven.

Cop off - *v* - Kiss.

Copper - *n* - Policeman.

Cor - *interj* - Ohhh!

Cor blimey - *interj* - Said to be an abbreviation of 'God Blind Me'. An interjection that has changed meaning over time. In early novels it was used in the same way as 'damn' to express exasperation or frustration. In recent years it is regarded as a mild expression of surprise or shock. Sometimes used to comic effect ('Blimey! It's the Rozzers!' - 'Goodness me! The police!'), in a deliberate reference to it being archaic usage.

Coriander - *n* - The herb cilantro.

Corrie - *n* - Short for Coronation Street - a soap opera aired on ITV.

Cot - *n* - Baby crib.

Cot death - *n* - SIDS.

Cotton buds - *n* - Cotton swabs.

Cotton wool - *n* - Cotton ball.

Council house - *n* - Public housing or a housing project.

Courgette - *n* - Zucchini.

Court shoes - *n* - Woman's high heeled shoe - a pump.

Cow - adj - A woman of contempt - a rude bitch.

Cowboy - n - A dishonest or incompetent trade worker.

Cream Crackered - *adj* - To be extremely tired.

Creche - *n* - Day-care or nursery.

Crikey - *interj* - General expression of surprise.

Crisps - *n* - Potato Chips.

Crumbs - *interj* - Another common expression of surprise.

Crumpet - *n* - A yummy teacake.

Crusty Dragon - *n* - A booger.

Cuppa - *n* - A cup of tea.

Current account - *n* - A checking account.

Cutlery - *n* - Silverware.

CV - *n* - Short for Curriculum Vitae but Americans would simply call it a Résumé.

D

Dab hand - *n* - To be particularly skilled at something.

Dabs - *n* - Fingerprints.

Daddy long-legs - *n* - Not to be confused with the type of spider, it actually refers to the crane fly.

Dado - *n* - A chair railing on a wall.

Daft - *adj* - An idiot, stupid, or foolish person.

Daft Cow - *adj* - A rude and stupid overweight woman.

Dago - *n* - Derogatory term for a Spanish, Italian or foreign person.

Damp - *n* - Mold or wet rot that is common in older homes.

Damp Squib - *adj* - An event which you think will be exciting but which actually turns out to be a disappointment.

Damper - *n* - The shock absorber on a car.

Dangly-bits - *n* - Male genitalia.

Dapper - *adj* - A well dressed and well spoken individual, can be used as a compliment or an insult.

Daylight robbery - *n* - A highway robbery.

Dear - *adj* - Something that is expensive or costly.

Dekko --n - A look, glance - to take a look at something.

De-mister - *n* - De-froster.

De-plane - *v* - To exit an aircraft.

Destroyed - *adj* - To be very drunk or intoxicated on drugs.

Diamond Geezer - *n* - A respected older gentleman, phrase mainly used in London.

Diary - *n* - A person's schedule or calendar. Not a personal journal.

Dibbles - *n* - Police officer as in Officer Dibble from Top Cat.

Diddle - *v* - To swindle or con someone.

Digestive - *n* - A biscuit that you dunk in your tea, sort of like a cookie that's supposed to aid in digestion.

Dim - *adj* - Someone who is stupid.

Div - *adj* - An idiot.

Divvy - *n* - An idiot.

DIY - *abbr* - Shorthand for Do it Yourself - i.e. for home improvement projects. "Fancy doing a little DIY this weekend?"

Do - *n* - A party.

Doddle - *n* - Something that is very easy.

Dodgems - *n* - Bumper cars.

Dodgy - *adj* - Something shady or rather dubious. Also can apply to something that was poorly made or doesn't work well.

Dog-end - *n* - A cigarette butt.

Dogging - v - The act of having sex in public parks while people watch.

Dog's bollocks - *n* - Something especially good is "the dog's bollocks".

Dog's breakfast - *n* - A complete mess.

Dog's Dinner - *n* - The same meaning as 'dog's breakfast'.

Dogsbody - *n* - A lowly servant or functionary

Dole - *n* - The various forms of welfare are lumped under this term. To be on the Dole is to live off the state.

Done Over - *v* - To be beaten up by someone.

Donkey's years - *n* - Something that happened a long time ago.

Dosh - *n* - Money.

Doss - *v* - To be lazy and not do much.

Double-barreled - *adj* - The practice of upper-class people having more than one last name joined together with a hyphen.

Dozy - *adj* - A person who is rather slow.

Draught - *n* - We say 'draft' as in a cold draft.

Draughts - *n* - The game of checkers.

Drawing-pin - *n* - A thumb tack.

Dressing gown - *n* - A bathrobe.

Dual carriageway - *n* - A divided highway a step down from a motorway.

Duff - *n* - Something that doesn't work.

Dummy - *n* - A baby's pacifier.

Dustbin - *n* - Garbage can.

Dustman - *n* - Garbage man.

Duvet - *n* - Bed cover.

Dux - *n* - The valedictorian at a school.

Dynamo - *n* - An electric generator.

E

Earner - *n* - A job that earns good money.

Easy Peasy - *n* - Something that is really easy to do.

Eating irons - *n* - Silverware/cutlery

Ecosse - *n* - The French name for Scotland.

Eejit - *n* - An idiot.

Effing - *adj* - A polite way to say 'f*cking.'

Egg Banjo - *n* - A fried egg sandwich.

Elastoplast - *n* - A band-aid.

Electrics - *n* - The electrical fittings in a house.

Elevenses - *n* - Means having a snack mid-morning.

End-piece - *n* - End of the male genitalia - another way of saying "bell-end."

Engaged - *adj* - To be busy with something.

Enplane - *v* - To get onto an airplane.

Entail - *n* - An old English custom that controlled how a large estate was inherited and what could be done with it.

Entrée - *n* - The appetizer portion of a meal.

Essex girl - *adj* - Derogatory term for a girl from Essex that does not have any class.

Estate agent - *n* - A realtor or real estate agent and generally they're not very respected.

Estate car - *n* - A station wagon.

Eurosceptic - *n* - A person who is against British involvement in the European Union.

Eurocrat - *n* - A derogatory term for the civil servants that work at the center of the European Union.

Ex-Council - *n* - An apartment or house that used to be public housing but has since been bought by the tenants (and perhaps sold on but it will always be known as ex-council).

Expat - *n* - Someone who lives abroad.

Eyetie - *n* - Someone from Italy - an offensive term.

F

Faff - *v* - To dither or screw around, pussyfoot around.

Fag - *n* - A cigarette.

Fag-end - *adj* - The used stub of a cigarette, and by extension the unpleasant and worthless loose end of any situation. "It was the Fag End of my shift, and I was knackered".

Faggot - *n* - A type of sausage.

Fairie cake - *n* - Also known to Americans as a cupcake.

Fairy lights - *n* - The general name for Christmas Lights.

Fancy - *v* - To desire or want to do something.

Fancy dress - *n* - To wear a costume.

Fancy dress party - *n* - A party where costumes are worn.

Fanny - *n* - A woman's vagina. Not for use in polite conversation.

Feck - *n* - An exclamation of anger of frustration similar to f*ck.

Filch - *v* - To steal something.

Flannel - *n* - Baby's washcloth

Flash - adj - Something that is showy or ostentatious.

Film - *n* - A movie. Brits would generally say they want to see a film not a movie.

Filth - *n* - A not so nice term for the police.

Fit - *adj* - A word used to describe an attractive woman or male.

Fitted - *v* - To have something installed.

Fiver - *n* - Five pounds sterling.

Fizzy drink - *n* - Soda-pop or soft drink.

Flag - *adj* - To be tired or lose all energy.

Flat - *n* - An apartment.

Flatmate - *n* - A roommate in your flat.

Flog - *n* - An attempt to sell something that may not be worth the money being asked.

Fluff - *n* - Dryer lint.

Flutter - *v* - A brief go at gambling.

Fly tipping - *v* - The act of dumping your trash in a place you're not supposed to.

Football - *n* - What Americans quaintly call soccer.

Football Pitch - *n* - A field where British Football is played.

Footie - *n* - A shorthand term for Football.

Footpath - *n* - A public path through the countryside for walking.

Fortnight - *n* - Two weeks. Often used in the UK when talking about time.

Freehold - *n* - Owning both the land and the building on the land. Sometimes in Britain a different person owns the land and the building. See 'leasehold'.

Freesat - *n* - A selection of free channels you can receive via satellite with a dish and a receiver.

Freeview - *n* - A selection of digital channels you can view for free if you purchase a Freeview receiver, which usually has added features.

Fringe - *n* - Hair bangs.

Fry-up - *n* - Another name for the full English breakfast as most of the meal is fried in some form.

Full English - *n* - A full English breakfast usually consists of eggs, sausage, black pudding, bacon, mushrooms, baked beans, hash browns, and half a tomato.

Full Monty - *n* - The entire take or everything that is desired.

Full stop - *n* - Period. The type at the end of a sentence.

Fun fair - *n* - Carnival or amusement rides.

G

Gaffe - *n* - A home.

Gaffer - *n* - The boss.

Gaffer tape - *n* - Duct tape.

Gagging - *v* - Desperate in a derogatory way. i.e. She was gagging for it.

Garden - *n* - Back yard.

Gash - *n* - Derogatory term used for the female genitalia.

Gatropub - *n* - A pub that serves food, sometimes pretentiously.

Gay - *adj* - Something that is bad, e.g. "It was 'gay' being mugged."

Gazump - *n* - To accept a higher offer on something at the last minute.

GCSE's - *n* - Academic tests that take place before the A-levels (many students stop here and 'graduate').

Gear lever - *n* - The stick shift in a manual car.

Gearbox - *n* - A car's transmission.

Geezer - *n* - Someone you respect.

Geordie - *n* - Someone from the Newcastle area. Made famous in Geordie Shore, a spin-off of MTV's Jersey Shore.

Get off - *v* - To make out with someone.

Get on - *v* - To do something. Commonly used in 'How did you get on?'

Get the Nod - *v* - To get permission to do something.

Get your end away - *v* - To have sex.

Giddy - *n* - To get dizzy or experience vertigo.

Ginger - *n* - A person with red hair.

Ginger beer - *adj* - Derogatory term for a homosexual.

Git - *n* - An incompetent, stupid, annoying, or childish person.

Give over - *interj* - To give up.

Give way - *interj* - To yield when driving.

Give You a Bell - *v* - Means to call someone on the phone.

Glop - *n* - Thick substance or unappetizing food.

Go - *v* - To try something. i.e. To give it a go.

Gob - *n* - Your mouth in a derogatory sense. Shot your gob!

Gobshite - *n* - Bullshit.

Gobsmacked - *adj* - Flabbergasted, dumbfounded, astounded, speechless.

Golf buggy - *n* - Golf cart.

Googly - *n* - A cricket ball that bounces around randomly when it lands.

Gone off - *v* - Something that's gone bad or expired.

Gormless - *adj* - Someone lacking in common sense.

Grammar - *n* - A textbook.

Grammar School - *n* - Elementary school.

Grand - *n* - Used in place of thousand (i.e. "This house is worth 140 grand").

Grass - *n* - A snitch.

Green fingers - *n* - Someone who is adept at the gardening arts.

Greenbelt - *n* - The land around cities and town in Britain that is left undeveloped to preserve the environment.

Greenfield - *n* - Land that can't be developed or built upon that's left to exist for the purpose of pretty landscapes.

GP - *n* - General Practitioner - your regular family doctor.

Grizzle - *n* - To grumble or moan, see whingeing. Also a fussy baby.

Grockle - *adj* - A derogatory term for a Tourist, primarily used in Southern England.

Grotty - *adj* - Something that is gross.

Growler - *n* - A very rude term for female genitals covered in pubic hair.

Guff - *v* - Fart.

Guinea - *n* - A older unit of currency that meant 1 Pound and 1 Shilling.

Gutted - *adj* - To be devastated or shocked about something.

Guv'nor - *n* - The boss.

Gyp - *n* - Something that's an irritating pain.

H

Hacked-off - *adj* - Annoyed or stressed.

Haggis - *n* - Legendary Scottish dish consisting of a sheep's minced heart, liver, and lungs cooked in its own stomach with onion, oatmeal, and spices.

Haha - *n* - Trench dug at the end of a garden in place of a fence to the view isn't spoiled.

Hand-luggage - *n* - Carry-on baggage.

Handbag - n - A woman's purse.

Handbags - *n* - A harmless fight

Handbrake - *n* - Parking/Emergency brake in a car.

Hard shoulder - *n* - Shoulder on the side of the road that's paved.

Hash - *n* - The # symbol.

Have a go - *v* - To give something a try.

Have a go hero - *n* - A person that attempts to defend their home or property against an intruder with force.

Haver - *n* - To ramble incoherently.

Having kittens - *interj* - To be extremely nervous.

Head boy - *n* - Highest achieving boy in a class similar to valedictorian.

Health and Safety - *n* - An all encompassing term of derision geared towards useless safety rules and regulations.

Helmet - *n* - 1. The glans of the penis 2. A fool.

Hen night - *n* - Bachelorette party.

Her Majesty's pleasure - *v* - To be put into prison.

Higgledy-piggledy - *adj* - Something all jumbled up or in disarray.

High street - *n* - Main street.

High tea - *n* - Late afternoon light meal that usually involves a cup of tea.

Hill-walking - *n* – Hiking.

Hire - *v* - To rent something. i.e. A hire car.

Hire car - *n* - A rental car.

Hob - *n* - A range or stove.

Hockey - *n* - Field hockey.

Holiday - *n* - What we would call a vacation or any time off of work. Brits usually get 28 days paid holiday. That's not a typo.

Hoodie - *n* - A young person usually known for their misdeeds who are identified by their distinctive clothing, a hooded sweatshirt.

Hoover - *n* - A vacuum cleaner.

Hoovering - *v* - The act of vacuuming.

Horses for Courses - *v* - To each his own.

Housing Estate - *n* - A sub-division but it can also mean a public housing estate as well.

Hum - *n* - A bad smell.

I

Icing sugar - *n* -
Powdered sugar.
Ickle - *n* - Something very
small.
Indicator - *n* - Turning
signal in a car.
Innit - *interj* - Shortened
from "ain't it" or isn't it.
Interval - *n* - Intermission
or a break in
performance.
Ironmonger - *n* - The old
name for a hardware
store.
Ivories - *n* - Teeth.

J

Jabs - *n* - Vaccinations or shots.
Jacket potato - *n* - A baked potato.
Jam - *n* - Jelly.
Jam sandwich - *n* - A term for Police Car.
Jammy - *adj* - Someone who is lucky.
Jammy dodger - *n* - A lucky person.
Jelly - *n* - What the British call Jell-O™, not to be confused with Jam, see above.
Jerry - *n* - Someone from Germany, derogatory.
Jim-jams - *n* - Pajamas
Jock - *n* - A Scottish person, usually male.
Jobsworth - *n* - An official who strictly adheres to rules and regulations. See Health and Safety.
John Thomas - *n* - Male genitalia.
Joint - *n* - A large piece of meat like a beef loin.
Jolly - *adv* - Very good.
Jollies - *n* - Pleasure or thrills.

Jubblies - *n* - A woman's breasts.
Jumble sale - *n* - A garage sale.
Jumped up - *adj* - Arrogant.
Jump leads - *n* - Car jumper cables.
Jumper - *n* - A sweater.

K

Kagoul - *n* - A poncho or windbreaker jacket.

Kecks - *n* - Pants or trousers.

Kerb - *n* - A curb.

Kerb crawler - *n* - A person who solicits street prostitutes.

Kerfuffle - *n* - To make a big fuss about something.

Kip - *n* - A word for sleep or to get some sleep (have a kip).

Kirby grip - *n* - Bobby pin.

Kit - *n* - Clothing or sports equipment.

Kitchen roll - *n* - Paper towel.

Kiwi - *n* - Someone from New Zealand.

Knackered - *adj* - Exhausted, tired, also 'broken'

Knackers - *n* - Vulgar name for testicles.

Knees-up - *n* - A party.

Knickers - *n* - Women's underwear, see pants.

Knob - *n* - Male genitalia.

Knob head - *adj* - A stupid, irritating person.

Knob jockey - *adj* - Homosexual, derogatory.

Knob-end - *adj* - An idiot, or tip of penis (see bell-end).

Knock about - *n* - Sporting practice.

Knock up - *v* - To bang on someone's door. Does not mean to impregnate.

Know your onions - *phrs* - To be very knowledgeable on a particular subject.

L

L-plates - *n* - Special license plates you're required to have on your car while learning to drive in the UK.

Lad - *n* - A boy or an immature grown male.

Laddette - *n* - An immature woman.

Ladybird - *n* - A ladybug.

Lager - *n* - A type of beer popular in England.

Lager lout - *n* - A person who misbehaves while drunk.

Lairy - *adj* - To be noisy or abusive.

Larder - *n* - Pantry.

Lav - *n* - Short for lavatory.

Lay-by - *n* - Rest area along the highways.

Leasehold - *n* - A possessory right to live in a building or flat but not owning the land upon which it sits. Common for apartments. Leases are usually for 99 or 999 years.

Left luggage - *n* - A place you can leave your luggage safely (for a fee) while you travel or shop.

Leg it - *v* - To run hurriedly.

Leg over - *n* - Sexual intercourse.

Lemonade - *n* - While in the UK if you ask for Sprite or 7-up you'll be given this which is basically carbonated lemonade.

Lie-in - *n* - The act of sleeping in.

Lift - *n* - An elevator.

Limey - *n* - An English person.

Local - *n* - The local pub.

Lodger - *n* - A person who rents a room in your home, lower on the scale than a flatmate.

Loft - *n* - The attic area of a house.

Lolly - *n* - A popsicle.

Loo - *n* - The bathroom.

Lorry - *adj* - A semi or heavy goods truck.

Lost the Plot - *n* -
Someone who's gone
mad.

Love - *n* - A kind form of
address ("Excuse me,
love").

Luv - *n* - Honey or
darling.

M

M and S - *abbr* - Shorthand for the department store Marks and Spencer's, the British equivalent to JC Penney. Also affectionately known as Marks and Sparks.

Macintosh - *n* - Light waterproof jacket, also known as a Mac.

Mad - *adj* - Crazy.

Made Redundant - *v* - Someone whose job no longer exists.

Maisonette - *n* - A set of rooms for living in, typically on two stories of a larger building and with its own entrance from outside.

Manc - *n* - Someone from Manchester.

Mancunian - *n* - A polite way to say someone is from Manchester.

Manky - *adj* - Dirty or filthy.

Manual gearbox - *n* - A manual transmission on a car.

Marmite - *n* - A strange spread usually eaten on toast made of yeast extract. An acquired taste often listed as one of the tops things Brits living abroad miss from home.

Marrow - *n* - The vegetable squash.

Mashed - *n* - High from smoking cannabis.

Mate - *n* - A good friend.

Maths - *n* - Mathematics. They say the S.

Meat and two veg - *n* - Male external genitalia.

Mental - *n* - Crazy or insane.

Mews - *n* - The short narrow street behind a house like an alleyway.

Mews house - *n* - Small house located on a mews street that often housed servants and horses but have since been converted into homes.

Miffed - *adj* - Pissed off.

Mileometer - *n* - A car's odometer.

Mince - *n* - Ground beef.

Mince pie - *n* - A sweet pie usually enjoyed at Christmas stuff with fruit and mincemeat (which is not actually meat).

Mind - *v* - To be aware of. "Mind the Gap."

Minge - *n* - Female genitalia, derogatory.

Minger - *adj* - An ugly or filthy-minded person. There is usually an implication of poor hygiene or body odor in the usage.

Minted - *n* - To be wealthy.

Mobile phone - *n* - We would say cell phone or cellular phone. Most Brits just say mobile.

Moggy - *n* - A cat.

Mole grip - *n* - Vise grip.

Molly-coddled - *adj* - To be overly looked after.

Mong - *n* - Derogatory term for someone with special needs.

Monged (out) - *n* - To be severely drunk or high.

Moose - *n* - A very unattractive woman

Moreish - *adj* - To want more of something.

Motor - *n* - An antiquated term for an automobile.

Motorway - *n* - The equivalent would be an interstate highway.

Move house - *v* - To move to a new house.

Multi-story car park - *n* - A parking garage.

Muck in - *v* - To help with or assist in something.

Muggins - n - A simple person or someone silly.

Mum - *n* - Mother.

Munter - *n* - An ugly person.

Muppet - *n* - An idiot.

N

Naff - *adj* - Something that tacky or otherwise in poor taste.

Nappy - *n* - Baby's diaper

Narked - *adj* - Being in a bad mood

Natter - *n* - Chatter.

Natty - *adj* - Cool.

Naughty bits - *n* - A polite way to say male genitalia.

Nause - *adj* - An annoying person.

Navvy - *n* - Road worker.

Nearside - *n* - The side of the car that's closest to the curb.

Newsagent - *n* - A convenience store where you can buy newspapers, magazines and snacks and drinks. Also known as a newsy.

Nick - *v* - To steal or arrest.

Nicked - *v* - To be arrested or something that was stolen.

Niggle - *v* - To pester.

Nimrod - *adj* - Another name for a weasel, but also used to called someone stupid.

Nip - *v* - To go off and do something quickly.

Nippy - *adj* - Cold.

Nob - *n* - A member of the nobility class.

Nonce - *n* - A pedophile.

Non-starter - *n* - An idea so absurd it has no chance of being a success.

Nosey parker - *n* - A person who gossips and won't mind their own business.

Nosh - *n* - Food.

Nought - *n* - The number zero. The Brits will almost never say zero.

Noughts and crosses - *n* - The game of tic-tac-toe.

Nowt - *n* - Nothing.

Number plate - *n* - License plate.

Numpty - *n* - An idiot.

Nutter - *n* - A crazy person.

O

O-levels - *n* - Series of exams that took place a few years before you're A-levels. Replaced the the GCSE's in the 1980's.

OAP - *Acronym* - Old Age Pensioner - someone living on social security.

Off one's onion - *adj* - Crazy.

Off one's rocker - *adj* - Crazy.

Off one's tits - *adj* - High on drugs.

Off one's trolley - *adj* - Crazy.

Off-license - *n* - An off license is a place where you can buy alcohol and other small household goods. I.e. the corner shop. Also known as the offie.

Offside - *n* - 1. The side of the car that is farthest from the curb. 2. Complicated rule in football that generates endless debate.

Oi - *interj* - Hey!

Old Bill - *n* - The police.

Old banger - *n* - An old crappy car.

OH - *n* - Other half - significant other.

Omnibus - *n* - 1. A gathering of a week's radio shows or a soap opera into one large episode. 2. What they used to call buses.

On the blink - *adj* - Something that doesn't work.

On the fiddle - *phrs* - Cheating.

On the piss - *v* - getting drunk, drinking alcohol.

On the pull - *v* - Out looking for sex.

One - *n* - Referring to yourself in the third person, The Royal We.

One Off - *n* - A special or one time event.

P

P45 - *n* - The form used when someone is being fired or made redundant.

P.A. - *n* - A personal assistant, secretary.

Pack it in - *v* - To give up.

Pantomime - *n* - A strange tongue and cheek play often performed at Christmas time that's popular with families. A panto has to be seen to be understood.

Pants - *n* - 1. Women's underwear. 2. Something that is total crap.

Paracetamol - *n* - The British equivalent to Tylenol.

Paraffin - *n* - Liquid kerosene.

Parky - *adj* - Cold or chilly.

Pastille - *n* - A type of small candy.

Pasty - *n* - A meat or vegetable filled pastry originating in Cornwall.

Patience - *n* - The card game of solitaire.

Pavement - *n* - The sidewalk.

Pear-shaped - *adj* - Something that's gone wrong.

Puckish - *adj* - To be a little hungry.

Peculiar - *adj* - Something that is unique.

Pedo - n - Shorthand phrase for pedophile.

Pelican crossing - *n* - A type of crosswalk on British streets.

Pensioner - *n* - An elderly person that's retired and collects their state pension.

Perspex - *n* - Plexiglass..

Pervy - *adj* - Perverted.

Petrol - *n* - Gasoline.

Phone box - *n* - Phone booth.

Phut - *adj* - Gone out, something that's stopped working.

Pig's ear - *n* - To make a mess out of something.

Pikey - *n* - A pejorative term used, mainly in England to refer to gypsies or people of low social class, offensive.

Pillock - *n* - An idiot.

Pimm's - *n* - A summery alcoholic drink popular in the UK.

Pinch - *v* - To steal.

Pint - *n* - A standard unit of drink measurement in the UK that's roughly equal to 20 ounces.

Pips - *n* - Seeds

Piss-artist - *n* - A lazy person.

Pissed - *adj* - Drunk

Pissed up - *adj* - Drunk

Pitch - *n* - Grassy surface suitable for football or cricket.

Plane-spotter - *n* - A person who hangs around airports and looks at airplanes.

Planning Permission - *n* - The process of getting a building permit in the UK, often involving several layers of government and approvals. Can take years.

Plaster - *n* - A band-aid.

Plastered - *adj* - Extremely drunk

Plasticine - *n* - A type of modeling clay used to make Wallace and Gromit.

Plimsolls - *n* - Canvas shoes with a rubber sole.

Plod - *n* - The police

Plonker - *adj* - An idiot.

Po-faced - *adj* - Glum.

Polo-neck - *n* - A turtleneck sweater.

Ponce - *n* - A homosexual, derogatory.

Pong - *n* - A bad smell.

Pongo - *n* - An infantryman in the military.

Porkies - *n* - Lies.

Portakabin - *n* - Pre-fabricated building often used as a temporary office.

Portaloo - *n* - Portajohn.

Posh - *adj* - Someone or something that is very high class.

Post - *n, v* - 1. The mail. To post something is to mail something. 2. The post is also your daily delivery of mail.

Postgraduate - *n* - A university level grad student.

Pot noodle - *n* - Ramen noodle soup.

Potholing - *n* - Spelunking.

Potplant - *n* - A potted plant.

Potty - *adj* - A little loopy or nuts.

Power Cut - *n* - An electricity black out.

Poxy - *adj* - Crappy.

Pram - *n* - Baby's stroller.

Prang - *n* - Minor car accident.

Prat - *n* - A particular type of idiot, jerk, or asshole.

Prawn - *n* - Shrimp.

Prefect - *n* - Head boy in a school.

Prep school - *n* - A type of boarding school for children.

Presenter - *n* - A radio or TV anchorperson.

Pub - *n* - Public house, the local bar.

Pub Grub - *n* - Simple food usually served in pubs or bars. Fish and Chips is a great example of Pub Grub. Differs from the type of food served in a gastropub, which is fancier.

Public school - *n* - Despite the confusing name, a public school is actually a private exclusive school like Harrow or Eton. Also called an 'independent school'.

Pudding - *n* - The dessert part of meal - not actual pudding.

Pukka - *interj* - The genuine article.

Pull - *v* - To have sex with someone.

Pump - *n* - Gym shoes.

Puncture - *n* - Flat tire.

Punt - *v* - To give something a try,

Punter - *n* - A customer or patron.

Purse - *n* - A little bag that holds change.

Pushchair - *n* - A child's stroller where the child sits upright.

Put paid - *v* - To settle a matter.

Q

Quango - *Acronym* - Quasi-autonomous non-governmental organization. An organization that's usually started by the government or has governmental powers that's not run by the government. It is usually a place to send troublesome politicians by giving them cushy jobs. Examples are the BBC and Visit Britain. See, TV show *Yes, Minister.*

Quay - *n* - A dock where boats are unloaded. Pronounced key.

Queue - *n, v, pron.* - A line or to stand in line.

Quid - *n* - 1 Pound Sterling (e.g. "That car only costs 500 quid.")

Quids-in - *n* - To be in profit or to be all in on something.

Quim - *n* - Female genitalia.

Quite - *n* - A general term that means 'kind of'.

R

Rag & bone man - *n* - A scavenger who makes value out of garbage.

Randy - *adj* - To be sexually aroused.

Rat-arsed - *adj* - Quite drunk.

Razz - *v* - Vomit.

Reckon - *adv* - To believe something is true.

Registration - *n* - A car's license plate.

Removal men - *n* - A moving company that helps you move house.

Return ticket - *adj* - A round-trip ticket.

Rent boy - *n* - A male prostitute.

Revise - *v* - To study.

Right - *adj* - To emphasize the meaning of something. "He was a right git."

Ring piece - *n* - The anus.

Rocket - *n* - Arugula salad.

Rodger - *v* - To have sex.

Romp - *v* - To have sex.

Ropey - *adj* - Something that's rather iffy.

Roundabout - *n* - A traffic circle.

Row - *n, pron* - An argument.

Rozzer - *n* - A police officer.

RSPCA - *Acronym* - Royal Society for the Prevention of Cruelty to Animals.

Rubber- *n* - An eraser (does not mean a condom).

Rubbish - *n* - 1. Garbage 2. A nicer way to say bullshit. 3. To criticize.

Runner - *v* - To run out on the bill at a restaurant.

Rucksack - *n* - Backpack.

S

Sack - *v* - To fire someone or be fired from your job.

Saloon - *n* - Standard 4 door family sedan car.

Samey - *adj* - Something that's similar.

Sarnie - *n* - Sandwich.

Savoury - *n* - Non-dessert food.

Scarper - *v* - To run away.

Scone - *n* - Buttery biscuit, usually served with tea with clotted cream and jam.

Scotch egg - *n* - A Scotch egg consists of a hard-boiled egg wrapped in sausage meat, coated in breadcrumbs and deep-fried.

Scouser - *n* - Someone from Liverpool.

Scrotty - *adj* - Dirty.

Scrubber - *n* - Someone who is dirty or perceived poor, an offensive term.

Scrummy - *adj* - Something that is delicious.

Scrumpy - *n* - Alcoholic apple cider.

Scupper - *v* - To obstruct.

Sectioned - *v* - To be committed to a mental health facility against your will.

See a man about a dog - *v phrs* - Attend a secret deal or meeting or to go to the toilet.

Sell-by-date - *n* - Expiration date (like on food).

Sellotape - *n* - Scotch tape.

Semi-detached - *n* - Usually a pair of houses that share a common wall and are mirror images of each other - a duplex. Also, called a 'semi' for short.

Sent down - *v* - To be sent to prison.

Septic - *n* - An American.

Serviette - *n* - Napkin.

Shag - *v* - To have sex.

Shambles - *adj* - A chaotic mess of something.

Shambolic - *adj* - Something in complete disarray similar to a shambles.

Shandy - *n* - A mixture of lager with Lemonade (see definition of lemonade.)

Shat - *n* - Another way of saying 'shit' but in the past tense.

Shattered - *adj* - To be emotionally devastated or extremely tired.

Shedload - *n* - A large quantity of something.

Shilling - *n* - A form of currency before Britain switched to the decimal that means five pence.

Shirty - *adj* - Irritable.

Shite - *n* - Shit.

Shop - *n* - A store.

Sick - *n* - The standard term for vomit or to throw up. "Oh man, I'm covered in sick."

Sickie - *n* - To take a day off of work or school but not actually be sick.

Skinfull - *n* - The amount of alcohol needed to make one drunk.

Skint - *adj* - To be broke.

Skip - *n* - Dumpster.

Skipping - *v* - Dumpster diving.

Skirting board - *n* - Baseboard.

Skive - *v, n* - To be lazy or take an unwarranted day off, pull a sickie.

Skivvies - *n* - Another word for underwear or undergarments.

Slag - *v* - A whore. To call a woman a slag is a grievous insult.

Slag off - *v* - To denigrate someone, start rumors, usually in the victim's absence.

Slap - *n* - Cosmetic make-up, used in a derogatory way to indicate the person is wearing too much.

Slap head - *n* - A bald man.

Slapper - *n* - A slut.

Slash - *v* - To urinate.

Sleeper - *n* - Railroad tie.

Sleeping policemen - *n* - A speed bump in the road.

Slip-road - *n* - An exit on/off ramp on a highway.

Smarties - *n* - A chocolate candy similar to M&M's but are unrelated to the American candy also called Smarties.

Smashing - *adj* - Awesome!

Smeg - *n* - Smeg is a vulgarism or expletive used throughout the TV Show *Red Dwarf*. Although no specific meaning is ever given, it and its derivatives are regularly used as a derogatory term.

Snakes and ladders - *n* - The board game chutes and ladder.

Snog - *v* - Passionate kissing, not sex.

Sod - *n, v, adj* - A idiot, moron, or annoying person.

Sod Off - *v* - To tell someone to 'piss off.'

Soft-Shoulder - *n* - Roadside shoulder that's made of gravel.

Soldiers - *n* - Little strips of bread used for dipping into a boiled egg.

Solicitor - *n* - A lawyer that deals with contracts and other personal legal matters and can represent clients in lower courts, not a barrister.

Sorted - *adj* - A problem that has been fixed.

Sound - *adj* - To be reliable or trustworthy.

Spanner - *n* - A wrench. Commonly used in the phrase to 'throw a spanner in the works' meaning to break something.

Spare - *adj, n* - 1. To be at one's wits end. 2. Used in reference to the younger sibling of the heir to the throne (i.e. Prince Harry).

Spastic - *n* - A very insulting and derogatory term for someone who is mentally challenged.

Speedo - *n* - British abbreviation for the speedometer - not to be confused with the article of clothing.

Spongle - *n* - Someone who is high on drugs.

Spotted dick - *n* - A type of spongecake with raisins in it.

Sport - *n* - The British say Sport as a plural instead of Sports.

Spot on - *adj* - Perfectly correct.

Spots - *n* - Pimples, zits.

Sprog - *n* - A young child.

Squiffy - *adj* - Something that's gone wrong.

Stabilisers - *n* - Training wheels on a bicycle.

Stag night - *n* - A bachelor party.

Starkers - *v* - To be completely naked.

Starter - *n* - The appetizer portion of a meal.

Steady on - *interj* - Hold your horses.

Steaming - *adj* - Extremely drunk, or extremely angry.

Sterling - *adj* - Awesome!

Stick - *n* - Walking stick or cane.

Sticking plaster - *n* - A band-aid.

Stockings - *n* - Ladies tights.

Stodgy - *adj* - Something that's old fashioned.

Stone - *n* - A strange unit of measure unique to Britain that measures 14 lbs usually used to measure the weight of a person.

Stonking - *adj* - Something really big.

Straight away - *interj* - Right away.

Strawberry Creams - *n* - A woman's breasts.

Strimmer - *n* - A weed-whacker.

Stroppy - *adj* - Unreasonably grumpy.

Stuffed - *v* - Sexual intercourse (i.e. 'get stuffed').

Subway - *n* - A pedestrian walkway located underground.

Sultana - *n* - A golden raisin.

Sun cream - *n* - Sunscreen.

Suspenders - *n* - Garters.

Suss - *v* - To figure something out.

Swede - *n* - Rutabega.

Sweets - *n* - Candy.

Swift half - *n* - A half pint of beer or lager.

Swimming costume - *n* - Bathing suit.

Swizz - *n* - A small con.

Swot - *n* - To cram for a test, to study hard.

T

Ta - *interj* - A simple thank you.

Tackle - *n* - Male genitalia.

Tad - *adj* - A little bit of something.

Take-away - *n, v* - 1. A fast food establishment. 2. To act of getting food and taking it home.

Taking the mickey - *interj* - Pulling one's chain.

Taking the piss - *n* - Mocking, taking advantage of someone.

Tally-ho! - *interj* - Goodbye!

Tannoy - *n* - Public Address (PA) system.

Tarmac - *n* - A paved road.

Tart - *n* - Prostitute or loose woman.

Tat - *n* - Cheap piece of junk, usually applied to souvenirs.

Tatty - *n* - A description for something that's tired and out of fashion. Like an old Seaside resort town.

Tea - *n* - Also known as tea-time, it's an evening meal.

Tea-break - *n* - Coffee break.

Tea-towel - *n* - A dish cloth.

Telly - *n* - Short for television.

Terraced Houses - *n* - A series of houses that line a street and all look the same.

Tetchy - *adj* - Irritable.

Thrupney bits - *n* - Woman's breasts.

Tick - *n* - To check something off on a list.

Tickety-boo - *adj* - When something is going smoothly or proceeding quickly.

Tights - *n* - Pantyhose.

Till - *n* - Check-out counter in a store.

Tip - *n* - A garbage dump or a place that's a mess.

Tippex - *n* - Whiteout or liquid paper (something that's rarely used much anymore).

Tipple - *n* - A civilized alcoholic beverage.

Titchy - *n* - Something that is very small.

Tits up - *adj* - Something that's gone all wrong.

Todger - *n* - Male genitalia.

Toe-rag - *n* - A total scumbag.

Toff - *n* - Someone who is from the upper classes, it's slightly derogatory.

Tomato sauce - *n* - Ketchup/catsup.

Top-up - *v* - To top off something, make it full or add to it.

Torch - *n* - Flashlight.

Tosh - *adj* - Nonsense.

Tosser - *adj* - A person who likes to pleasure themselves but generally used as an insult against an idiot.

Touch-up - *v* - To feel up or grope.

Trailer tent - *n* - A pop-up camper.

Train-spotter - *n* - A person who stands around waiting for interesting trains.

Trainers - *n* - Gym shoes.

Tram - *n* - A streetcar - basically a bus on rails.

Tramp - *n* - Homeless person.

Travellers - *n* - A group of people who travel around Britain and live in makeshift campsites - often illegally, modern day Gypsies. Sometimes called Irish Travellers, but they're not always Irish. They're universally hated by everyone as they often cause a blight on the landscape.

Treacle - *n* - Molasses.

Trilby - *n* - A type of men's hat.

Trolley - *n* - A shopping cart in a store.

Trollop - *n* - A woman with loose morality.

Trolly dolly - *n* - Air stewardess, derogatory.

Trots, the - *n* - Diarrhea.

Trousers - *n* - Pants/slacks.

Tube - *n* - The London Underground.

Twee - *adj* - Something that's quaint.

Twig - *v* - To catch on to something.

Two up, two down - *n* - A house with two rooms downstairs and two rooms upstairs, popular in Victorian times.

Twonk - *n* - An idiot.

Tyke - *n* - A rascally child.

Tyre - *n* - How the British spell tire.

U

Undercarriage - *n* - 1. Male or female genitals. 2. The underside of your car.

Underground - *n* - Usually refers to the London Underground but there are other underground subway systems in the UK.

Uni - *n* - Short for University or College

University - *n* - Even if they're going to a college, the post-secondary school part of their educational career is called University. Going to university, when I was at university, etc.

Up for it - *phrs* - To be up to doing something - enthusiastic about it.

Up the duff - *v* - To be pregnant.

Uphill gardener - *n* - A homosexual, derog.

V

VAT - *Acronym* - Value Added Tax. Essentially a 20% sales tax on pretty much everything.

Verge - *n* - Shoulder on the side of the road.

Vest - *n* - Piece of clothing worn under your shirt.

Video - *n* - What the British called a VCR.

Village green - n - Common land at the center of a village where people can play Cricket or Football.

Vino - *n* - Poor quality inexpensive wine.

W

WAG - *Acronym* - Stands for 'Wives and Girlfriends' and is related to the women who are involved with Football players. Slightly derogatory as it indicates the type of woman attracted to that type of lifestyle.

W.C. - *n* - Watercloset, which is a lavatory.

Waffle - *n* - To ramble or waste time talking about a subject.

Waistcoat - *n* - A vest.

Wally - *n* - An unintelligent person.

Wank - *v* - To masturbate.

Wanker - *adj* - Literally someone who enjoys to masturbate but usually used as an insult for an asshole.

Washing up - *n* - To do the dishes.

Washing up liquid - *n* - Dishwashing soap.

Waster - *n* - A Time waster or lazy person.

Way out - *n* - An exit. Often used instead of the word exit.

Wazzack - *n* - An idiot.

Wellingtons - *n* - A type of waterproof rubber boot commonly worn in the countryside. Shorthand version is 'wellies.'

Wedding tackle - *n* - Male genitalia.

Wendy house - *n* - A small children's playhouse.

Whinge - *v* - To moan or whine about something. You pronounce the g.

Whip round - *n* - Passing the buck.

White van man - *n* - A general term for contractors or home repairmen who usually travel around in an unmarked white van.

Whittling - *v* - To urinate in public.

Whitworth - *n* - Someone keen on classic.

Wholemeal flour - *n* - Whole grain wheat flour.

Whovian - *n* - A fan of the British science fiction TV show *Doctor Who*.

Wicked - *adj* - Something really cool.

Wind - *n* - When one farts or has bad gas.

Windscreen - *n* - Windshield.

Wing - *n* - Car fender.

Wizard - *adj* - Something really cool.

Wobbler - *n* - A fit of anger.

Wobbly - *n* - Something that's not quite right.

Wonga - *n* - Another word for Money from the African term.

Wonky - *adj* - Something that's not quite right.

Woolly - *adj* - Something that's not well defined.

Wretch - *v* - To throw up/vomit.

Y

Y-fronts - *n* - Men's
undergarments.
Yank - *n* - Generally
how Brits like to refer
to Americans.
Yob - *n* - A young
hooligan, usually
identified by wearing
a hood.
Yonks - *n* - A long
time.
Yummy Mummy - *n* -
A young, good
looking mother.

Z

Zapper - *n* - TV remote
control.
Zebra crossing - *n* -
Pedestrian crossings on
roads.
Zed - *n* - The British
pronounce the letter Z as
'zed.' They don't say
'zee.'

British Insults

While we generally covered what is and isn't an insult in the main dictionary, we thought it'd be useful for quick reference to summarize all our favorite insults in one place. This is not an exhaustive list by any means.

Tosser - Supreme asshole or jerk.
Wanker - Idiot or someone who enjoys to masturbate.
Slag - Whore, the worst kind.
Cheese Eating Surrender Monkeys - The French.
Lost the plot - Gone crazy or completely stupid.
Daft Cow - Dumb, large woman.
Arsehole - Asshole.
Barmy - Stupid or crazy.
Chav - Low Class trash.
Dodgy - Something that's shady or doesn't work well.
Git - Moron, Idiot.
Gormless - Complete lack of common sense.
Manky - Disgusting.
Minger - Very unattractive woman.
Muppet - Dimwit (not the puppet variety).

Naff - Tacky.
Nutter - Someone's who's clearly crazy.
Pikey - Used to slight Gypsies or Irish. Travellers.
Pillock - Idiot.
Plonker - Idiot.
Prat - Idiot, asshole.
Scrubber - A nicer way to say slag.
Trollop - A lady of questionable morals.
Uphill Gardener - Another way of saying homosexual.
Twit - Idiot.
Knob Head - Dickhead.
Piss Off - Go Away.
Bell End - Dick Head (bell end also means penis).
Lazy Sod - Useless idiot.
Skiver - Lazy sod.
Knob - Dick.

Wazzock - Someone so dumb they can only do manual labor (from Yorkshire).

Ninny - Brilliant but inferior.

Berk - Idiot.

Airy-fairy - Not strong, weak.

Ankle-biters - Children.

Arse-licker - A sycophant.

Arsemonger - A person that generate contempt.

Chuffer - An annoying perfusion.

Daft as a bush - Silly, Crazy.

Dead from the neck up - Stupid.

Gannet - Greedy person.

Gone to the dogs - rotten, deteriorated.

Ligger - Freeloader.

Like a dog with two dicks - Man whore.

Mad as a bag of ferrets - Crazy.

Maggot - A despicable person.

Mingebag - A bad person, an asshole who might be cheap.

Not batting on a full wicket - Eccentric person. a little crazy or odd.

Plug-Ugly - Very Ugly person.

London Slang

One thing you'll notice when you travel to London is all the different words they use to describe things. Sometimes they make sense, sometimes they don't. We thought it would be useful to put together a list of words you'll usually only hear in London. So, here's your guide to some useful London Lingo.

Tube - London Underground Network.

The Knowledge - The cumulative knowledge of London's black cab drivers that they have to learn to be licensed. They have to learn every street in London.

BoJo - Boris Johnson, the current mayor of London.

Boris Bike - The bikes located in various places around London that you can rent by the half hour.

Boris Bus - Boris Johnson's key platform of replacing the old London Routemaster bus.

Red Ken - The name of London's former Mayor Ken Livingston who leaned VERY far to the left.

The Standard - What some call the Evening Standard - the evening paper dedicated to London.

The City - The City of London - the square mile bit of central London that goes back 2 thousand years.

Square Mile - Physical boundary of the City of London.

Congestion Charge - Tax on all cars entering the central London congestion charge zone.

Silicon Roundabout - Area around Old Street that's a hub for new media and tech companies.

Council Estate - Public housing.

The Blitz - Period in 1940 when London was bombed by the Nazis.

M25 - The Orbital Highway that encircles London.

Westway - Elevated Highway in West London.

Mind the Gap - Watch your step when stepping from a train to a platform on the Tube.

The Palace - When someone says the Palace they're almost always referring to Buckingham Palace, the Queen's official residence in London.

Buck House - Buckingham Palace.

The Tower - Tower of London.

A-Z - A popular London map guide that's indispensable to locals and long term visitors (extra note - Londoners will say 'A to Zed').

GMT - Greenwich Mean Time.

Cockney - Someone born within earshot of the bells of St Mary-le-Bow.

Offy - Convenience Store that also sells alcohol.

Off License - Convenience Store that also sells alcohol.

Take Away - Cheap food to go.

Crossrail - New cross London underground railway line currently under construction.

Bobby - London Policeman

Clip Joint - A club that claims to be a strip club but usually comes with £100 bottles of water. Avoid.

Zebra Crossing - Pedestrian crossing.

Home Counties - Generic name for the counties around London which are: Bedfordshire, Berkshire, Buckinghamshire, Cambridgeshire, Dorset, Essex, Hampshire, Hertfordshire, Kent, Middlesex, Oxfordshire, Surrey and Sussex.

Nappy Valley - Areas of London with high birthrates like Battersea.

The Big Smoke - Another term for London.

Oyster Card - A electronic card used to pay for the Tube without a paper ticket. Often you get a cheaper fare this way.

Cockney Rhyming Slang

Cockney Rhyming Slang is believed to have originated in the mid-19th century in the East End of London, with sources suggesting sometime in the 1840s. The Cockney population are well-known for having a characteristic accent and speech patterns.

It remains a matter of speculation whether rhyming slang was a linguistic accident, a game, or a secret language developed intentionally to confuse non-locals. If deliberate, Cockneys may also have used it to maintain a sense of community. It is possible that it was used in the marketplace to allow vendors to talk amongst themselves in order to facilitate collusion, without customers knowing what they were saying. Another suggestion is that criminals may have been used it to confuse the police.

What follows is a list of words that rhyme, but also a list of words commonly used by Cockney speakers.

A

Adam and Eve - Believe.
Afters - Short for the term 'after hours'.
Agro - Short for violence.
Alan Whicker(s) - Rhyming Slang for 'knickers'.
All over the gaff/shop - Someone that's in a mess.
Allright / awright - Greeting that means 'is everything all right?'
Apples and pears - Stairs.
Artful Dodger - Lodger.
Ascot Races - Braces.
Aunt Joanna - Piano.
Ayrton Senna - Rhyming Slang for 'tenner'.

B

Backhander - A dodgy payment.
Baked Bean - Queen.
Baker's Dozen - Cousin.
Ball and Chalk - Walk.
Ballistic - To go mad.
Banged up - To be put in prison.
Bangers - Another name for sausages.
Banjaxed - Meaning drunk or stoned.

Barmy - A mad person.
Barnaby Rudge - Judge.
Barnet Fair - Hair.
Barney - Violent argument.
Barney Rubble - Trouble.
Battlecruiser - Boozer.
Bean flicker - A lesbian.
Beer monster - A laddish heavy drinker.
Bees and honey - Money.
Bell - A telephone call.
Bender - A drinking spree, or a gay bloke.
Bent - Stolen.
Bent as a nine bob note - Illegal.
Bimbo - A young woman considered sexually attractive but of limited intelligence.
Bird lime - Time in prison.
Bit of awright - Used by men to refer to an attractive young lady.
Blinder - Amazing or wonderful.
Blow-off - Fart.
Blower - Slang for telephone.
Bluey - Pornographic video.
Bo Peep - Rhyming Slang for 'sleep'.
Boat Race - Face.

Bob Hope - Rhyming Slang for 'dope'.

Borasic lint - Rhyming Slang for 'skint'.

Bottle - Courage.

Bottle and glass - Arse.

Botty boy - Offensive slang for gay man.

Bovver - Fighting.

Brahms and Liszt - Pissed (drunk).

Brass Tacks - Facts.

Bread - Rhyming slang for 'money'.

Bread and Cheese - Sneeze.

Bread and Honey - Money.

Bricks and Mortar - Daughter.

Bristol City - Breasts.

Brown Bread - Dead.

Bubble and Squeak - Greek.

Bubble Bath Laugh.

Bun in the oven - Meaning pregnant.

Bunk-off - To be absent without permission.

Bunk-up - Sexual intercourse.

Butcher's hook - A look.

C

Cabbage - Bit slow or foolish.

Cabbaged - Used for tired of drunk.

Cack - Rubbish.

Cakehole - Mouth.

Caned - Drunk or stoned.

Carpet muncher - Lesbian.

Chalfont St. Giles - Piles.

Chalk Farm - Arm.

Char / cha - Tea.

Charlie - Cocaine.

Chief - Used to address a man.

China - Rhyming Slang, short for 'China plate', 'mate'.

China plate - Mate (friend).

Chip - To leave.

Choked - Very disappointed.

Chronic - Terrible.

Chutney ferret - Gay man.

Claire Rayner's - Rhyming Slang for 'trainers'.

Claret - Slang for blood.

Cobblers - Rhyming Slang, short for 'cobblers awls', 'balls'.

Cock and bull story - A rubbish story.

Cock and Hen - Ten.

Cop shop - Police station.

Cows and Kisses - Missus (wife).

Crack - Something that is a laugh.

Crikey - Astonishment.

Crust - Money.

Currant bun - Sun (also The Sun, a British newspaper).

Custard and jelly - Telly (television).

D

Daisy Roots - Boots.

Darby and Joan - Moan.

Dead cert - Definite.

Diamond geezer - A reliable person.

Dicky bird - Word.

Dicky Dirt - Shirt.

Diesel dyke - A butch lesbian.

Diggs - Lodgings.

Ding-dong - Argument.

Dinky Doos - Shoes.

Dodgy - Dubious person.

Dog and bone - Phone.

Dog's dinner - Overdressed.

Dog's meat - Feet [from early 20th c.].

Done over - Beaten up.

Doris - A woman who is plain.

Dosh - Money.

Dosser - Tramp.

Double bubble - Double time.

Duck and Dive - Skive.

Duke of Kent - Rent.

Dustbin lid - Kid.

E

Elephant's Trunk - Drunk.

Emma Freud's - Rhyming Slang for hemorrhoids.

Extracting the urine - Taking the piss.

F

Family jewels - Rhyming Slang for 'balls'.

Farmer Giles - Rhyming Slang for 'piles'.

Fireman's Hose - Nose.

Float an air biscuit - To fart.

Flowery Dell - Cell.

Folding - Paper money.

Fridge and freezer - Rhyming Slang for 'geezer'.

Frog and Toad - Road.

Funny farm - Mental hospital.
Funny money - Counterfeit money.

G

Geezer - A man.
Ginger beer - Rhyming Slang for queer.
Gone for a Burton - Rhyming Slang for 'to leave'.
Goolies - Balls, testicles.
Gooner - An Arsenal fan.
Goppin' - Ugly or disgusting in some way.
Gordon Bennet - An exclamation.
Got the nod - To receive approval.
Gregory Peck - Rhyming Slang for 'neck'.
Guv'nor or guv - Meaning 'boss'.
Gypsy's kiss - Piss.

H

Hacked off - Fed up, annoyed.
Had it away on his toes - To run away quickly.
Half-inch - Pinch (to steal).
Hammered - Drunk.

Hampstead Heath - Rhyming Slang for 'teeth'.
Hampton Wick - Prick.
Hank Marvin - Starving.
Herbert - A foolish person.
Hole in the wall - Cashpoint machine.
Holy Ghost - Rhyming Slang for 'toast'.
How's your father - A euphemism for sex.

I

In stook - In trouble.
Irish pig - Wig.
Isle of Wight - Tights.

J

Jack Jones - Rhyming Slang for 'own'.
Jam-jar - Car.
Jazz mag - Pornographic magazine.
Jimmy Riddle - Piddle.
Joanna - Piano (pronounced 'pianna' in Cockney).
Johnny-bag - Condom.
Juiced / juiced up - Very drunk.

K

Keep your hair on - Keep calm.
Khyber Pass - Arse.
Kick and Prance - Dance.
Kick it off - Start a fight.
Knocking shop - Brothel.

L

Lady Godiva - Fiver.
Laugh n a joke - Smoke.
Leave it out - Stop doing that.
Leg-over - To have sexual intercourse.
Leggit - Run away fast.
Legless - Very drunk.
Lionel Blairs - Flares.
Loaf of Bread - Head.
Loop the loop - Soup.
Lost the plot - Gone crazy/mad.
Luvvly jubbly - That all is well.

M

Manor - Territory, area, turf.
Mickey Bliss - Piss.
Mince Pies - Eyes.
Minging - Drunk, disgusting.

Missus - Bit of a lad's term for the wife.
Nonkey - A term for £500.
Moolar - A slang term for money of uncertain origin.
Mork and Mindy - Windy'.
Motor / motah - A car.
Mug / muggins - A fool or victim.
Muppet - A foolish or stupid person.
Mutt 'n Jeff - Rhyming Slang for deaf.
Mystic Meg(s) - Rhyming Slang - for 'legs'.

N

Nadds, nadgers - Testicles.
Naff - Cheap and nasty.
Naff off - "Go away".
Night out on the tiles - A late night out, usually drunk.
Nipper - A small child.
Nonce - A sex offender.
North and south - Mouth.
Notes - A term used to mean money in general.
Nugget - A pound coin.

O

Off your face - To be drunk.
Off your trolley / rocker - A bit mad, crazy.
Oily (rag) - Rhyming Slang for cigarette.
Old fruit - An affectionate address.
On the game - To be prostitute.
On the job - To be involved in sexual activity.
Orchestra stalls - Balls.
Out of your tree - Crazy, drunk or stoned.

P

Pan handle - An erection.
Pat and Mick - Sick.
Pear-shaped - It has gone wrong.
Peckham Rye - Tie.
Pen and ink - Rhyming Slang for 'stink'.
Pete Tong - Rhyming Slang for 'wrong'.
Pictures of the Queen - Paper money.
Plates of meat - Feet.
Pony - Slang term for £25.
Pony and Trap - Crap.

Porky pies - Rhyming Slang for 'lies'.
Powder your nose - Taking cocaine.

R

Rabbit (rabbit and pork) - Rhyming Slang for 'talk'.
Radio Rental - Rhyming Slang for 'mental'.
Raspberry ripple - Nipple.
Raspberry tart - Fart.
Rat-arsed - Drunk.
Roast Pork - Fork.
Rosy Lee - Tea (drink).
Round the Houses - Trousers.
Rub-a-Dub - Pub.
Ruby Murray - Curry.
Rug - Wig, toupee.

S

Sausage Roll - Goal.
Scarpa / scarper - Rhyming Slang for 'to run off'.
Scrounge - To beg or sponge.
Septic tank - Yank.
Sexton Blake - Rhyming Slang for 'fake'.

Shagged-out - To feel tired.

Shed-load - A huge amount.

Shell-like - The ear.

Shell-out - To have to pay for

Sherbert dab - Rhyming Slang for 'cab'

Skin and Blister - Sister

Skin diver - Rhyming Slang for 'fiver'

Skint - To have no money

Skirt - Young attractive woman.

Sky Rocket - Pocket

Spliff - Common term for a cannabis cigarette.

Spondulics - Money.

Steffi (Graff) - Rhyming Slang for 'laugh'.

Steve Mcqueen's - Rhyming Slang for 'bake beans'.

Stuffing - To perform sexual intercourse.

Stunner - A very good looking bird.

Sweeney Todd - Flying squad.

Syrup of figs - Wig (sic).

T

Tables and chairs - Stairs.

Tea leaf - Thief.

That old chestnut - See chestnut.

The nick - Police station, or prison.

Thrupenny bits - Rhyming Slang for 'tits'.

Tits-up - All gone wrong.

To go down - Sent to prison.

Todd Sloane - Alone.

Tom and Dick - Sick.

Tomfoolery - Jewelry.

Tommy Trinder - Window.

Trouble and strife - Wife.

Trouser action - A general euphemism for sexual activity.

Two and eight - State (of upset).

U

Uncle Tom Cobley and all - Everyone.

V

Vera Lynn - Gin.

W

Weasel and stoat -
Rhyming Slang for
'coat'.
Well ard/hard - Someone
or something that is very
tough.
Whistle and flute - Suit
(of clothes).
Wind up - To tease, to
perform a prank.
Wind-up merchant -
Someone who
specializes in teasing.
Wonga - Money.

Scottish English Words

Here is a list of common Scottish English words and phrases. This is not meant to be an exhaustive list but an overview of the most commonly used phrases.
Generally, words that are used commonly throughout the rest of Britain have been excluded from the list.

A

Auld - Old.
A-wiz-nae - I was not.
A, ah - I.
Aboot - About.
Aff - Off (off yer heed).
Ah ya bastart - Ouch, that hurt.
Am no - I am not.
Am ur - I am.
Am-ur-nay - I am not.
An empty - The residents who live in the house are not present and people take advantage by having a party in the "empty" house.
Anno - I know.
Arse / erse - Bum.
As-laat - "I was like that"; i.e., I was remarked to say.
Awrite - Alright.
Aye - Yes.

B

Bairn - Baby.
Bltic - Really cold (It's baltic!).
Bampot - An idiot, unhinged person (He is a bampot).
Barras - A short slang term for a place called the Barrowland in the east end of Glasgow.
Bastirt - Bastard, also a term of endearment.
Bawbag - Scrotum, pejorative (That guy's a bawbag).
Bawhair- A recognized unit of measurement.
Baws - Testicles.
Bevvy - Drink.
Bisom - 'Ya wee bisom' which means difficult women, spoilt bratty girl.
Blether - Inane chat.

Bletherskite - To talk rubbish.
Blootered - Drunk.
Boaby - Police. Can also mean penis (She's pure gettin the boaby the night!!).
Boak - To throw up.
Bobee - 6 pence in old money.
Boggin - Smelly, dirty (That's boggin'!).
Bolt - Go away ("wanty bolt!").
Bonglie - Highlanders call tourists 'Bonglies.'
Boot - Ugly woman (Shut it, ya boot!).
Bowfin - Smelly.
Brassic - Skint.
Braw - Beautiful.
Breek - Trousers.
Burd - Girlfriend/Boyfriend.
Burn - Small river (Let's awa' up that burn).

C

Cannae - Can not.
Cannie - Careful (caw cannie be careful).
Chapel - Catholic church ("I am going to chapel on Sunday").

Claes - Clothes.
Clatty bint - Dirty girl.
Cludgie - Toilet.
Crabbit - Crab.
Cummoan - Lets go.
Cushie - Meaning pigeon.

D

Dafty - Silly.
Dancin - Nightclub.
Dead - Usually used with "pure" in front to describe something (That's pure dead brilliant!!!).
Diddy - Did he?
Dinnae - Don't ("Dinnae dae that!").
Dobber - A fool/stupid person. Also means "dickhead" ("Whit ye daein ya dobber?!").
Donner - A walk (comin fur a wee donner doon yonder?).
Doon - Down.
Dreich - Cold as in it's a driech day outside.
Dug - A dog.
Dunderheed - A nice fool.

E

Dejit - Idiot.

F

Dae - From (a ken where yur dae).
Feert - To be scared, afeared (I'm feert of the dark).
Fitbaw - Football.
Fizzog - Face.
Fud - A complete and utter dobber .

G

Gadgie - An old man.
Gan - Go.
Gantin - Smelly/really wanting something.
Geggy - Mouth.
Gingin (pronounced "ging-in") - Disgusting .
Glaikit - A fool.
Glasgow Kiss - A headbutt.
Glesga - Glasgow.
Bobble - Blowjob.
Gomeril - Fool.
Gonnae no dae that - Please do not do that.
Gowpin - Sore body part.
Gran - Grandmother.

Granda - Grandfather.
Guay strangy bairn - Meaning a baby's nappy needs changing!
Gutties - Gym shoes/Trainers.

H

Haar - Fog.
Hackit - Ugly.
Hame - Home "am away hame."
Haud your wheest - Quite.
Hauf ' - A measure of whiskey.
Hawd - Hold, stop "wanty hawd that?"
Hawd yer wheeshd - Stop talking.
Hawn - Hand "watch ma hawn."
Heed/heid - Head "a've got a sare heed."
Honkin - Smelly/dirty.
Hoose - House "it's in ma hoose."
How? - Why?
Howfin/howlin - Smelly.

I

I dinnae ken - Don't know.

J

Jag - An injection.
Jake(y) - A homeless or unkempt person (usually describing an alcoholic).
Jaked - Being in a state of drunkenness (I was jaked last night).
Jessie/jessy - Wimp/big girl's blouse.
Jobby - Poo; plural form "jobbies."

K

Ken - Term for the word 'know.'

L

Lang - Surname.
Lecky - Electricity - often used in reference to bills (she didn't pay her lecky this month).
Liftit - To be arrested by the police.
Loaby - Hallway, lobby, passageway.
Loch - Lake.
Loupin - Cry sore/infested with lice ("My heid is loupin.").

M

Magic - Great/excellent.
Maist - Most.
Maw - Mum (Aye yer maw).
Mawkit/ manky - Very dirty (Your trousers are mawkit!! Ya manky wee bam!!).
Meltit/melted - To be stoned on drugs - (Ah was pure melted man!).
Mibay - Maybe.
Minted - Rich/wealthy ("Look at his motor, he must be minted.).

N

Nae danger - No problem ("Ye want mince and totties fur yur dinner? Nae danger").
Napper - Head.
Naw - No.
Ned - Acronym for 'non-educated delinquent', useless waster, troublemaker.
Neeps – Mashed turnips.
Nip - Kiss a single measure of an alcoholic spirit, often whisky.
Nippin - Stinging.

Numpty - A useless individual/moron.
Nut - 1. Head 2. Or another term used for the word no.

O

Oaf - Off.
Oan yer bike - Go away.
Oan yer trolley - Go away.
Oot - Out.
Outwith - Outside.

P

Pan - Break or disfigure ("pan the windows in").
Peely wally - Pale or pasty.
Pish - Piss.
Pished - Drunk.
Polis - The police.
Pure - Very, totally ("she's pure no right".) used to emphasis something.

Q

Quality - Great/excellent ("That film was quality.").

R

Radge - A fit of rage.
Roamin - Taking a walk.

S

Scheme - Residential area usually council estate.
Scooby - Clue, (no clue).
Scramble - Go away.
Scunner - One who pisses you off.
Scunnered - To be pissed off.
Scunnurt - Fed up (Ah'm pure scunnurt).
Shite - Shit.
Shneck - Kiss.
Shneeb - Smoke.
Shoogle - To take.
Skelp - To smack or hit someone/thing.
Skiddies - Gentleman's undergarments with traces of last nights dinner.
Skuddy - Naked.
Solid - Hard, tough.
Sook - Big softie (ya wee sook).
Squint - Not straight.
Steamin - Drunk.
Stramash - A disturbance, a noisy racket, or a crash

Swallae - To swallow, also means alcohol.

T

Talking oot yer fanny flaps - Lying.

Tan - Smash windows (I'm gonny tan yer windaes).

Tanned - To drink/drunk or to vandalize.

Tap - To borrow money from someone.

Tatties/tatters - Potatoes.

That's a sin - What a shame.

Toaty - Small/tiny.

Tube - An idiot/fool.

Turkish - A piece of poop.

Twally - A person of lesser intellect.

W

Waldies - Wellies.

Wan - One (number or referring to an object or person).

Wean - (pronounced "Wayne") - Child.

Wee small - A child.

Willy – A man's penis.

Y

Yer erse is oot the windae - You are revealing your bottom.

Yin - One (not the number but referring to a person or object).

West Country English

Here is a sampling of several popular and obsolete words and phrases common in the English West Country. Some of these words may sound familiar from the hit British TV show Doc Martin. We indicate with each word where it's primarily spoken.

Acker (North Somerset, Hampshire, Isle of Wight) - Friend.

Alaska (North Somerset) - I will ask her.

Allernbatch (Devon) - Old sore.

Alright me ansum (Cornwall & Devon) - How are you, my friend?

Alright me babber (Somerset) - Similar to Alright me ansum.

Alright my luvver (just as with the phrase alright mate, when said by a person from the West Country, it has no carnal connotations, it is merely a greeting. Commonly used across the West Country).

Anywhen (Hampshire, Isle of Wight) - At any time.

Appen (Devon) - Perhaps, possibly.

Arable (Devon, Dorset, Somerset, Wiltshire and the Isle of Wight) - (From horrible), often used for a road surface, as in Thic road be arable.

Bad Lot (North Somerset) - E.g. They'm a bad lot, mind.

bauy, bay, bey (Exeter) - Boy.

Beached Whale (Cornwall) - Many meanings, most commonly used to mean a gurt grackle.

Benny (Bristol) - To lose your temper (from a character in Crossroads).

Billy Baker (Yeovil) - Woodlouse.

Bodmin (Cornwall) - Gone crazy.

Boris (Exeter) - Daddy longlegs.

Cheerzen/Cheers'en (Somerset, Bristol) - Thank you (from Cheers, then).

Chinny reckon (North Somerset) - I do not believe you in the slightest (from older West Country English ich ne reckon 'I don't reckon/calculate').

Chine (Isle of Wight) - Steep wooded valley.

Chuggy pig (North Somerset) - Woodlouse.

Chump (North Somerset) - Log (for the fire).

Chuting (North Somerset) - (pronounced shooting) Guttering.

Comical (North Somerset, Isle of Wight) - Peculiar, e.g. 'e were proper comical.

Combe (Devon, Isle of Wight) (pronounced 'coombe') - Steep wooded valley.

Coombe (Devon, North Somerset, Dorset) - Steep wooded valley. Combe/Coombe is the second most common placename element in Devon and is equivalent to the Welsh cwm.

Coupie or Croupie (North Somerset, Dorset, Isle of Wight & Bristol) - Crouch, as in the phrase coupie down.

Crowst (Cornwall) - A picnic lunch, crib.

Cuzzel (Cornwall) - Soft

Daddy granfer (North Somerset) - Woodlouse.

Daps (Bristol, Wiltshire, Dorset, Somerset, Gloucestershire) - Sportshoes (plimsolls or trainers) (also used widely in South Wales).

Diddykai, Diddycoy, Diddy (Isle of Wight, Hampshire) - Gypsy, Traveller.

Dimpsy (Devon) - Describing the state of twilight as in 'it's getting a bit dimpsy.'

Dreckley (Cornwall, Devon, Somerset & Isle of Wight) - Soon, like mañana, but less urgent (from directly once in common English usage for straight away) I be wiv 'ee dreckley.

Drive (Bristol, Somerset & Wiltshire) - Any driver of a taxi or bus. The usual gesture when disembarking from a bus is cheers drive.

Emmet (Cornwall and North Somerset) - Tourist or visitor (derogatory).

Gallybagger (Isle of Wight) - Scarecrow.

Geddon (Crediton, Devon) - Get on, e.g. 'geddon chap!'

Gert Lush (Bristol) - Very good.

Gleanie (North Somerset) - Guinea fowl

Gockey (Cornwall) - Idiot.

Gramersow (Cornwall) - Woodlouse.

Granfergrig (Wiltshire) - Woodlouse.

Grockle (Devon, Dorset, Somerset, Wiltshire and the Isle of Wight) - Tourist, visitor or gypsy (derogatory).

Grockle Shell (Devon, Dorset, Somerset, Wiltshire and the Isle of Wight) - Caravan or motor home (derog).

Gurt (Cornwall, Devon, Somerset, Dorset, Bristol, South Glos and the Isle of Wight) - Big or great, used to express a large size often as extra emphasis That's a gurt big tractor!

Haling (North Somerset) - Coughing.

(H)ang'about (Cornwall, Devon, Somerset, Dorset, Hampshire & the Isle of Wight) - Wait or Pause but often exclaimed when a sudden thought occurs.

Hark at he (Hampshire, Isle of Wight)(pronounced 'ark a' 'ee) - Listen to him.

Headlights (Cornwall) - Light-headedness, giddiness.

Hilts and gilts (North Somerset) - Female and male piglets.

Hinkypunk - Will o' the wisp.

Hucky duck (Somerset, particularly Radstock) - Aqueduct.

Huppenstop (North Somerset) - Raised stone platform where milk churns are left for collection — no longer used but many still exist outside farms.

Ideal (Bristol) - Idea. In Bristol there is a propensity for local speakers to add an l to words ending with a.

Janner (Devon, esp. Plymouth) - A term with various meanings, normally associated with Devon. An old term for someone who makes their living off of the sea. Plymothians are often generally referred to as Janners In Wiltshire, a similar word ' jidder ' is used — possible relation to 'gypsy'.

Janny Reckon (Cornwall and Devon) - Derived from Chinny Reckon and Janner, and is often used in response to a wildly exaggerated fisherman's tale.

Jasper - A Devon word for wasp.

Keendle teening (Cornwall) - Candle lighting.

Kimberlin (Portland) - Someone from Weymouth or further away — not a Portlander.

Madderdo'ee (Cornwall) - Does it matter?

Maid,(devon,exeter) - Girl.

Maggoty (Dorset) - Fanciful.

Mackey (Bristol) - Massive or large, often to benefit.

Mang (Devon) - To mix.

Nipper (Isle of Wight) - A young boy, also a term of endearment between heterosexual men used in the same way as 'mate'.

Now we're farming (Somerset) - Term to describe when something is proceeding nicely or as planned.

Old butt (Gloucestershire, Forest of Dean) - Friend.

Ooh Arr (Devon) - Multiple meanings, including Oh Yes. Popularised by the Wurzels, this phrase has become stereotypical, and is used often to mock speakers of West Country dialects. In the modern day Ooh Ah is commonly used as the correct phrase though mostly avoided due to stereotypes.

Overner (Isle of Wight) - Not from the Island, a mainland person. Extremely common usage.

Parcel of ol' Crams (Devon) - A phrase that sums up and dismisses things that cannot be comprehended or believed.

Piggy widden (Cornwall) - Phrase used to calm babies.

Plimmed, -ing up (North Somerset) - Swollen, swelling.

Poached, -ing up (North Somerset) - Cutting up, of a field, as in the ground's poaching up ,we'll have to bring the cattle indoors for the winter.

Proper job - (Devon, Cornwall, West Dorset, Somerset, Isle of Wight) Something done well

Pummy (Dorset) - Apple pumice from the cider-wring .

Scag (North Somerset) - To tear or catch ("I've scagged me jeans on thacky barbed wire. I've scagged me 'ook up 'round down 'by Swyre 'ed").

Scrage - A scratch or scrape usually on a limb BBC Voices Project.

Slit pigs (North Somerset) - Male piglets that have been castrated.

Smooth (Bristol & Somerset) - To stroke (e.g. cat or dog).

Somewhen (Isle of Wight) - At some time (still very commonly used).

Sprieve (Wiltshire) - Dry
after a bath, shower or
swim by evaporation.

Spuddler (Devon) -
Somebody attempting to
stir up trouble. e.g.
That's not true, you
spuddlin' bugger!

Thic (North Somerset) -
That — said knowingly,
i.e. to be make dialect
deliberately stronger.

Wambling (Dorset) -
Wandering, aimless
(see A Pair of Blue
Eyes by Thomas Hardy)

**Wuzzer/wazzin
(Exeter)** - Was
she?/Was he?

Where's it to? - Where is
it? (Devon,Dorchester,
where's it to? It's in
Dorset.)

Young'un - Any young
person 'Ow be young
un? or where bist goin'
youngun?

Zat (Devon) - Soft.

Yorkshire English

Yorkshire English is spoken in the countryside in the North of England and we've put together a short list of words so help you translate. This will be useful when watching a show like All Creatures Great and Small.

'Appen - Perhaps, maybe.
'Ard on - Fast asleep.
'As-ta - Have you.
'At - That.
'Eck - Hell.
'Od - Hold.
'Od on - Wait.
'Oil - Hole, doorway, place.
'Oss - Horse.
'Ouse - 1. Sitting room 2. House.
'Ummer - Heck (NB always used with the and not t').
Aboon - Above.
Addle - Aarn.
Afower - Before.
Agate - To do something.
Agin - Again.
Ah - I.
Alike - Similar.
Allicker - Vinegar.
Allus - Always.
Apiece - Each.
Arran - Spider.
Ax - Ask.
Aye - Yes.

Backend - Autumn.
Backword - To break an agreement or arrangement, cancel.
Bahn - Going/been.
Baht - Without.
Bairn - Child.
Band - String.
Bawl - Cry.
Beck - Stream.
Belong - Come from.
Belt - Hit hard.
Biddy - Louse.
Bide - 1. Wait 2. Like 3. Put up with.
Blowed - Amazed.
Blubberin' - Crying.
Blue murder - Trouble.
Bob - To go ie, just bobbin' out.
Boskin - Stone/wooden/concrete division between tied up cows.
Brass - Money.
Brossen - 1. Full (after a meal) 2. Big headed.
By gum - By God.

Ccack 'anded - 1. Left handed 2. Clumsy.
Capped - Surprised.
Champion - Excellent.
Chimbly/chimly - Chimney.
Chuffed - Proud.
Chump - 1. Gather wood for Bonfire Night 2. Wood.
Chunter - Grumble.
Coil - Coal.
Cop - Catch.
Cumly - Good looking.
Cup - Rose.
Cut - Canal.
Daft - Stupid.
Dahn - Down.
Dee - Die.
Delf - Quarry.
Din - Noise.
Doff - Take off (referring to clothing).
Don - Put on (referring to clothing).
Dooar 'oil - Doorway.
Durns't - Dare not.
Een - Eyes.
Egg on - Encourage.
Et/etten - Ate/eaten.
Fadge - To move with a gait between a jog and a trot.
Fair - Quite.
Feckless - Useless (person).

Fettle - 1. Work 2. Fix 3. Condition.
Flag - Paving stone.
Flaggin' - Tiring.
Flibberty gibbet - Chatterbox.
Flippin' - A mild expletive eg. flippin' 'eck.
Flit - To move house.
Flummox - To confuse.
Fo'ty - Forty.
Forced - Necessarily (used in the negative eg. not forced to be - not necessarily).
Foss - Waterfall.
Fower - Four.
Frame - Shape up (frame yer sen', lad - shape up boy).
Fratch - A fight.
Fresh - 1. New 2. Slightly drunk.
Fust - First.
Gaffer - Boss.
Gallivant - Travel around.
Gallock - Left.
Gallusses - Trouser braces.
Gammy - 1. Injured, lame 2. Bad, off (food).
Ganzy - Pullover.
Gawp - Stare.
Gear - Clothes.
Gerr away - You don't say.

Gill - Half a pint.

Gimmer - 1. Young female sheep 2. An insult (eg. Y'owd gimmer - You silly old person).

Ginnel - Narrow passage between buildings.

Gip - To nearly vomit.

Gob - Mouth.

Gob smacked - Lost for words.

Goit - A small artificial channel carrying water.

Gommeril - Fool.

Goose gogs - Gooseberries.

Gormless - 1. Not intelligent 2. Accident prone.

Grand - Fabulous, very nice, great.

Gumption - Common sense.

Gurt - Big.

I' - In.

Idle - Lazy.

Int' - In the.

Jiggered - Tired.

Jip - Pain.

Kayli - Sherbet.

Keak - To jerk a limb or tilt the head.

Kedge - A glutton.

Kets - Manure spread on a field.

Kist - Chest.

Kit - Milk pail.

Knackers - Testicles.

Lahl - Tittle.

Laik - Play.

Laithe - Barn.

Lame - Painful.

Land - To hit (ie, Ah'll land one on yer - I'll hit you).

Leet - Light.

Lern - Teech.

Let on - Tell.

Lig - Lay (eg, John's ligged out - John's lying down).

Lip - Answer back.

Lowsin' time - Home time.

Lug - 1. Ear 2. Carry.

Mad allik - Reckless.

Maddled - Confused.

Manky - Off (as in food), dirty, smelly.

Mardy - Bad mood.

Mashin' - Brewing a pot of tea.

Mend - Getting healthier.

Mi - Me.

Middlin' - Average.

Mind - Take care (eg, mind yer sen' - take care of yourself).

Missen - Myself, me.

Mistal - Cow shed.

Mother - To bother or harass someone.

Muck - Dirt.

Muck 'oil - Dirty room/house.
Mun - Must.
Na then - 1. Hello 2. Watch it.
Nantle - To fidget or rearrange.
Nay - No.
Neb - Nose.
Nivver - Never.
Nobbut - Only.
Nowt - Nothing.
Offcumden - A person from somewhere else.
Owd - Old.
Ower - Over.
Owt - Anything.
Parkin - A type of ginger cake common at bonfire night.
Parlour - Sitting room.
Pawse - Kick.
Pize - To hit someone.
Quacken - To cure.
Rawk - Thick fog.
Real - Outstanding.
Reckon - Believe.
Reek - Bad smell.
Reet - 1. Right 2. Very.
Reight - Right.
Rive - Tear.
Room - Sitting-room.
Rue - Regret.
Sam up - Gather.

Scunner - North Yorkshire term for an urban youth and usually associated with trouble or petty crime.
Seg - Metal stud for shoes.
Sen - Self.
Sharp - Quick.
Shun - Ignore.
Sickened - Upset.
Side - Clear up.
Sile - Rain heavily.
Sin - Since.
Sitha - See thee here.
Sithee - 'See here'.
Skeg - Glance, look.
Slack - Slow when referring to work/business.
Snap - Packed lunch.
Soft - Weak, cowardly, stupid.
Soz - Sorry.
Spice - Sweets.
Stalled - Bored.
Starved - To be cold.
Suited - Pleased.
Summat - Something.
Sup - Drink, sip.
T' - To.
Tarra - Goodbye.
Teem - Pour heavily as in rain eg. it's teemin' dahn.
Tha'/thou - You.
Think on - Remember.
Thissen - Yourself, you.

Thoil - To be able to
  justify the expense of a
  purchase.
Thy - Your.
Thysen - Thyself.
Touched - Simpleton.
Tyke - 1. Yorkshireman 2.
  Dog.
Umpteen - A lot.
Unheppen - Clumsy.
Us - Me/my or our.
Usen' - Ourselves.
Wahr - Worse.
Waint - Won't or
  wouldn't.
Wang - Throw.
Watter - Water.
Wed - Married.
Wekken - To wake.
While - Until.
Wi - With.
Wuthering - Blustery,
  windy.
Y' - You.
Yon - That over there.
Yonder - Over there.
Yorksher - Yorkshire.
Yure - Your.

Scouse English

Scouse English is primarily spoken in the Merseyside area of England and it's closely associated with the city of Liverpool and it's surrounding areas. The Scouse accent is highly distinctive, and has little in common with those used in the neighboring regions of Cheshire and Lancashire. A nickname for some from this area is simply as 'scouser.' Here is a selection of words unique to Scouse English.

'ad off - Someone else's poor fortune.

'ang on a mo' - please wait a moment.

'ave off - a spot of improvised good fortune.

'ar 'ey - Oh no!

Arl arse - Cruel.

Arl Fella - Father

Auld baig - Old woman. pron; Owld baig.

Az if - I don't believe that.

Bail - Go Away.

Beaut - An idiot

Better beaut - An extreme idiot

Bevied up - Drunk.

Bevvy - Beer

Bifter - A cigarette or joint

Bizzies, 'de - The Police.

Blag - Lie.

Blaggin' me 'ead - Lying to me.

Blert - A lightweight. Usually from down south.

Blind scouse - Vegetarian version of the scouse national dish.

Bombed out church, de' - St. Luke's.

Boss - Very good.

Butty - Sandwich.

Clobber - Clothes.

Cocky, de' - Night watchman.

Come 'ead - Lets go. Lets do it.

Crocky - Croxteth district. North end.

de' - The.

Deffo - Definitely.

Divvy - A stupid person.

Do one - Go away.

Echo, 'de - Liverpool's evening newspaper that is written and staffed by fools.

Fat Wap - An overweight person.

Gary Ablett's - Ecstasy tablets.

Geggin' in - To join in on something when you aren't invited.

Giz - Give.

Gobshite - Annoying Person or someone who does something stupid.

Is right - I agree.

Is wrong - An argumentative response to is right.

Jarg - counterfeit, fake, poor quality.

Jerk in bed - Birkenhead; a town on the wrong side of the River Mersey.

Jigger - 1. A girocheque. 2. A back alleyway.

Kidder - See la'.

Knock off - Stolen goods.

Knowsley - Officially not Scouseland.

Kopite - LFC (Liverpool Football Club) fan.

La' - Lad.

Lid - See la'.

Made up - Very happy about something.

Manc - A lowly cotton mill worker.

Meff - A smelly, badly dressed person.

N' dat - Something else.

No need - An exclamation of disapproval.

Noggsy - Norris Green district of the city. North end.

North End, de' - North end of the city eg. Noggsy, Crocky, de' Brook, Walton.

On one - To act in a reckless manner.

On top te fuck - A bad situation.

On you - Staking a claim for next go on a spliff.

Ozzy, de' - Hospital.

Paddy's Wigwam - The Catholic Cathedral.

Plazee Scouser - A person who adopts a Scouse accent and mannerisms in attempt to appear cool.

Posh twat - Someone from certain areas of the south end or from down south.

Probe - Legendary Liverpool record label and record store.

Professional Scouser - eg. Jimmy Tarbuck, Cilla Black, Stan Boardman.

Rocket - Beginning and end of the M62 motorway.

royal'ozzy - The Royal Hospital.

Sack it la' - Stop that. Don't do it.

Sayers pastie - Scousers lunch.

Scally - Archetypal Liverpool youth.

Scratch - Signing on the dole.

Shanks - The legendary Bill Shankly.

Skag Head - Heroin addict.

Slotted a boss hatrick - Scored 3 goals.

Soft Lad - Friendly name for a fool.

Sou-ey - Southport, an affluent and small former resort town north of the city. Famous for being robbed blind during English Bank Holidays.

South End, de' - South end of the city eg. Aigy, Speke, Garston see Mud Man, Allerton.

Sozz - Sorry.

Speke - Airport now re-branded as John Lennon International. Also district. South end.

Swerve on it - Not bother with it.

Ta' - Thank you.

Tellin' ye' - Emphasizing agreement.

Texan - A beaut with a high opinion of him/herself.

Tocky - Toxteth district of the city. South end.

Trabs - Sports shoes.

Wabs - Ganja.

Whopper - An idiot.

Woolyback / Wool - A person from Runcorn, Wirral, Wigan, Warrington, Southport etc.

Ye ma - Your mother.

Ye wha? - Pardon.

Yez/Youz - You (plural).

You'll Never Walk Alone - LFC anthem. Show tune popularized by Gerry and his ferry.

Funny British Place Names

Britain is a land of geographic linguistic variety, with some names going back thousands of years, this leads to amusement when a name from long ago means something completely different in the modern era. With that said, here's our list of amusing places names located throughout the United Kingdom.

London

- Back Passage, London
- Mincing Lane, London
- Mudchute, London
- Percy Passage, London
- Swallow Passage, London
- Trump Street, London
- Cumming Street, London
- Cockfoster, London
- Dick Turpin Lane, London
- Cock Hill, London
- Titley Close, London
- Cockbush Avenue, London

England

- Acock's Green, Worcestershire
- Babes Well, Durham
- Bachelors Bump, Essex
- Backside Lane, Oxfordshire
- Balls Green, Kent, England
- Balls Cross, WestSussex
- Bareleg Hill, Staffordshire
- Barking, Essex
- Beaver Close, Surrey
- Bedlam Bottom, Hampshire
- Beef Lane, Oxfordshire
- Beer, Devon

- Beggars Bush, Sussex passed her prime
- Bell End near Lickey End
- Bishops Itchington, Staffs
- Bitchfield, Lincolnshire
- Boggy Bottom, Abbots Langley, Herts
- Booty Lane, NorthYorkshire
- Bottoms Fold, Lancashire
- Broadbottom, Cheshire
- Brown Willy, Cornwall
- Bushygap, Northumberland
- Catholes, Cumbria
- Catsgore, Somerset
- Charles Bottom, Devon
- Clap Hill, village in Kent
- Clay Bottom, Bristol
- Cock Alley, Calow
- Cock Bridge, Hope, Derbyshire
- Cock Green, nr Braintree
- Cock Lane, Tutts Clump, Berkshire
- Cock Law, Northumberland
- Cock and Bell Lane, Suffolk
- Cockermouth, Cumbria
- Cockernhoe, nr Luton
- Cocking, Midhurst, West Sussex
- Cockintake, Staffordshire
- Cockpit Hill, Derbyshire
- Cockplay, Northumberland
- Cocks, Cornwall
- Cockshoot Close, Oxfordshire
- Cockshot, Northumberland
- Cockshutt Wood, Sheffield
- Cockup Lake District, Cumbria. UK
- Coldwind, Cornwall
- Crackington Haven, Cornwall, UK
- Crackpot, North Yorkshire
- Crapstone, Devon
- Crotch Crescent, Oxford
- Deans Bottom, Kent
- Devil's Lapful, Northumberland

- Dicks Mount, Suffolk
- Drinkstone, Suffolk
- Faggot, Northumberland
- Fanny Barks, Durham
- Fanny Avenue, Derbyshire
- Fanny Hands Lane, Lincolnshire
- Feltham Close, Hampshire
- Feltwell, Norfolk
- Fingringhoe, Essex
- Flesh Shank, Northumberland
- Friars Entry, Oxfordshire
- Fruitfall Cove, Cornwall
- Fudgepack upon Humber, Humberside
- Gay Street, Sussex
- Gays Hill, Cornwall
- Giggleswick, Staincliffe, Nth. Yorkshire
- Golden Balls, Oxfordshire,
- Gravelly Bottom Road, nr Langley Heath, Kent
- Great Cockup & Little Cockup, hills in The Lake District
- Great Horwood, Bucks
- Great Tosson, Northumberland
- Grope Lane, Shropshire
- Hampton Gay, Oxfordshire
- Happy Bottom, Dorset
- Helstone, Cornwall
- Hole Bottom, Yorkshire
- Hole of Horcum, North Yorkshire
- Holly Bush, Ledbury, Herefordshire
- Honey Knob Hill, Wiltshire
- Honeypot Lane, Leicestershire
- Hooker Road, Norwich
- Horncastle, Linconshire
- Horneyman, Kent
- Hornyold Road, Malvern Wells, UK
- Horwood, Devon
- Jeffries Passage, Surrey
- Jolly's Bottom, Cornwall
- Juggs Close, EastSussex

- Knockerdown, Derbyshire
- Letch Lane, Bourton-on-the-Water, The Cotswolds
- Lickar Moor, Northumberland
- Lickers Lane, Merseyside
- Lickey End, Worcestershire
- Lickfold, West Sussex
- Little Horwood, Bucks
- Little Bushey Lane, Hertfordshire
- Long Lover Lane, Halifax
- Lower Swell, Gloucestershire
- Menlove Avenue, Liverpool
- Minge Lane, Worcestershire
- Moisty Lane, Staffordshire
- Nether Wallop, Hampshire
- Nob End, South Lancashire
- Nork Rise, Surrey
- North Piddle, Worcestershire
- Ogle Close, Merseyside
- Old Sodbury, Gloucestershire
- Old Sodom Lane, Wiltshire
- Over Peover, Cheshire
- Pant, Shropshire
- Penistone, Sth Yorkshire
- Piddle River, Dorset
- Pork Lane, Essex
- Pratt's Bottom, Kent
- Prickwillow, Cambridgeshire
- Pump Alley, Middlesex
- Ram Alley, Wiltshire
- Ramsbottom, Lancs
- Rimswell, East Riding of Yorkshire
- Sandy Balls, Hampshire
- Scratchy Bottom, Dorset
- Shaggs, Dorset
- Shingaycum Wendy, Buckinghamshire
- Shitlingthorpe, Yorkshire
- Shitterton, Dorset
- Shittington,, Bedfordshire
- Six Mile Bottom, Cambridge
- Slackbottom, Yorkshire

- Slag Lane, Merseyside
- Slip End, Beds
- Slippery Lane, Staffordshire
- Snatchup, Hertfordshire
- Spanker Lane, Derbyshire.
- Spitalin the Street, Lincolnshire
- Splatt, Cornwall
- Staines, Surrey
- Stow cum Quy, Cambridgeshire
- Swell, Somerset
- The Blind Fiddler, Cornwall
- The Bush, Buckinghamshire
- The Furry, Cornwall
- The Knob, Oxfordshire
- Thong, Kent
- Tinkerbush Lane, Oxfordshire
- Titcomb, near Inkpen, Berkshire
- Titlington Mount, Northumberland
- Titty Hill, Sussex
- Titty Ho, Northamptonshire
- Tosside, Lancashire
- Turkey Cock Lane, Colchester, Essex

- Ugley, Essex
- Upper Bleeding, Sussex
- Upper Chute, Hampshire
- Upper Dicker & Lower Dicker, East Sussex
- Upperthong, West Riding, Yorkshire
- Wash Dyke, Norfolk
- Weedon Lois, Northampton
- Weedon, in the Parish of Hardwick, Buckinghamshire
- Weeford, Staffordshire
- Wet Rain, Yorkshire
- Wetwang, East Yorkshire
- WhamBottomLane, Lancashire
- Wideopen, Newcastle
- Willey, Warwickshire
- Winkle Street, Southampton
- Wormegay, Norfolk

Scotland

- Ardfork, Aberdeenshire
- Ardgay, Ross & Cromarty
- Assloss, Ayrshire
- Backside, Aberdeenshire
- Backside, Banffshire
- Ballownie, Angus
- Blackdikes, Angus
- Bladda, Paisley
- Forest Dyke Road, Lanarkshire
- Boghead, Ayrshire
- Boysack, Angus
- Brokenwind, Aberdeenshire
- Butt of Lewis, Hebrides
- Cock of Arran, Isle of Arran
- Cumloden Court, Dumfries and Galloway
- Dick Court, Lanarkshire
- East Breast, Inverclyde
- Fannyfield, Ross and Cromarty
- Fattiehead, Banffshire
- Hillo'ManyStanes
- Inchbare, Angus
- Inchinnan Drive, Renfrewshire
- Inchmore, Aberdeenshire
- Merkins Avenue, West Dumbartonshire
- Stripeside, Banffshire
- Tarty, Aberdeenshire
- The Bastard, a mountain in Scotland
- Twatt, Orkney

Wales

- Bullyhole Bottom, Monmouthshire
- Cat's Ash, Monmouthshire
- Pant-y-Felin Road
- Penisarwaen, village in Gwynedd
- Sodom, Flintshire
- Splott, Cardiff
- St.Mellons, Cardiff
- Stop-and-Call, Pembrokeshire
- Tarts Hill, Flintshire
- Three Cocks, Breconshire

Australian English

Here's a quick guide to Australian English slang words. You'll definitely see the influences of American and British English on Australian Slang but you'll also see words that mean something completely different than you think. It's a fun list!

A

Ace - Excellent, very good.

Aggro – Aggressive or aggravation.

Apples, she's - Everything is all right; often modified with will as in she'll be apples.

Arsey - Someone showing daring, audacity, and/or cheekiness.

Not being arsed - Lack of interest, as in "I couldn't be arsed to do it". Also British English.

Arvo - Short for afternoon; in use since the 1950s.

As if - Exclamatory rejection. "As if they're real tears!" or "The case was dismissed? As if."

Aussie salute - Brushing away flies with the hand.

B

B & S - In full Bachelors' and Spinsters' Ball - a party/function held for young single people.

Bag - (v) To denigrate; (n) An ugly woman; both senses in use since the 1960s.

Bags - To reserve, as in "(I) Bags the last frosty fruit (ice block)" or "Can someone do the dishes?" "Bags not!"

Bail (somebody) up - To corner somebody.

Bang - Sexual intercourse.

Barkers eggs - Dog poo.

Beaut - Great, fantastic, terrific.

Beauty - Exclamation showing approval, often spelt as bewdy.

Beef - To have a problem with someone.

Bickie - Biscuit. Sometimes also used as a word for a cigarette lighter, after the manufacturer Bic.

Big bickies - Lots of money.

Big-note oneself - To brag or boast.

Bizzo – Business.

Biff or biffo - A brawl or fist fight.

Bitser - Dog of mixed parentage, mongrel.

Blow - A rest, especially after physical work.

Bloody - Very (bloody hard yakka).

Bloody oath - That's certainly true; used as an affirmative to a statement.

Blue - A fight, brawl or heated argument or an embarrassing mistake.

Bluey - Formerly, a bundle of belongings wrapped in a blanket carried by swagmen.

Bludge - To shirk, be idle, or waste time either doing nothing or something inappropriate.

Bodgy - Of inferior quality.

Bog in - Commence eating, to attack a meal with enthusiasm.

Bog standard - Basic, unadorned, without accessories .

Bomb - An old mechanically unsound car. "That car is a bomb."

Bonzer - Great, ripper.

Boogie board - A hybrid, half-sized surf board.

Boong - A term lately considered highly derogatory, used for Australian Aboriginals.

Bottler - Something excellent.

Brumbie - Wild (as in undomesticated) horse.

Buck's night - Stag party, male gathering the night before the wedding.

Buggered (1) - Tired. "I'm feeling buggered."

Buggered (2) - Broken, not in working order. "That hose is buggered."

Buggered (3) - In trouble, or caught out. "I was caught speeding, I'm buggered!"

Built like a brick shithouse - Being strongly built.

Bundy - A nickname for a brand of rum (Bundaberg Rum).

Bung - Originally a stopper in a cask; a synonym for "put" or "place"; as in "bung it in the oven" or not working, broken, impaired, injured or infected.

Bung it on - To put on a show of pretence.

Bush - Woodland, generally called bushland, rural Australia.

Bush bashing - To force a path through the bush either by bushwalking or driving a 4WD (SUV) or the like.

Bush bash - A long competitive running or motorcar race through the bush.

Bushfire - Wild forest fire.

Bushie - A person living in remote rural areas,

Bush oyster - A gob of expelled nasal mucus.

Bush telly – Campfire.

Bushman's hanky - Emitting nasal mucus by placing one index finger on the outside of the nose (thus blocking one nostril) and blowing.

Bushwalking - Hiking in the bush.

Buttsucker - Someone who smokes cigarettes.

C

Cackleberry - Egg

Cactus - Dead, non-functional, not functioning.

Cark it - To die or to cease functioning.

Carn - Assimilation of "come on!" or "Go on!"; usually used to either goad someone.

Cat's pyjamas or cat's whiskers - Something great or perfectly suited, as in.

Cattle duffer - A cattle rustler.

Chook - A chicken.

Chrissie - Christmas

Chuck a sickie - Take the day off sick from work when you're perfectly healthy.

Chunder - Vomit. "I had a chunder."

Clayton's - Fake, substitute, not the real thing, ersatz.

Clucky - Feeling broody or maternal.

Cockie – Farmer; also short for 'cockatoo', an Australian bird.

Come a gutser - Make a bad mistake, have an accident.

Compo - Workers' compensation pay.

Cossie, cozzie - Swimming costume, bathers.

Cranky - In a bad mood, angry.

Crikey - An exclamation of surprise.

Crook - Angry, in the phrase "go crook at", sick or unwell, unfair.

Crunk - To get drunk.

Culosis - A resigned expression of frustration.

Cut - angry or upset.

D

Dag - An unfashionable or uncool person, equivalent to "geek" or "dork".

Daggy - Unfashionable, uncool, "nerdy", "dorky."

Darl - Term of endearment usually used for one's spouse: shortening of darling.

Dead set - (adj) Certain; indisputable; (adv) Completely "You're dead set right about that."

Deadly – Excellent.

Devo - Devastated or deviant.

Der - That's obvious, duh.

Derro - A term for idiot , someone who is stupid, or has done something ridiculous.

Deso - The designated driver on a night out.

Dekko - A look, to inspect something.

Dink - To give somebody a lift on the back of a bicycle.

Dinger – Condom.

Dinkum - Honest, genuine, real.

Dinky-di - The real thing, genuine.

Dirty - Bad, when applied to weather.

Division - Electoral district, equivalent to constituency in UK.

Dob - To inform on. To "dob (somebody) in" is to inform on somebody.

Docket - A bill, receipt.

Doco – Documentary.

Doona - British duvet. From the brand name Doona.

Drongo - Foolish person.

Drum - Information, tip-off ("I'll give you the drum.").

Duchess – Sideboard.

Duck's nuts, duck's guts or bee's knees - Something that is perfectly suited.

Dummy - A device, usually plastic, for babies to suck. cf. American pacifier.

Dummy, spit the - Get very upset at something.

Dunny – Toilet.

Dux - Top of the class (n.); to be top of the class (v.).

E

Earbashing - Nagging, non-stop chatter.

Emu bob - The duty given to enlisted men in the military, of picking up cigarette butts lying around barracks and parade grounds.

F

Fair dinkum - True, genuine; see dinkum.

Fair enough - I don't see a problem with that; OK.

Fair go or fair crack of the whip - A chance or a reasonable opportunity to complete a task.

Fair shake of the sauce bottle - A request to cut the speaker some slack, used as a preface to a statement.

Fair suck of the sav - Exclamation of wonder, awe, disbelief.

FBT - A large truck, "fucking big truck."

Feral - A derogatory term for variety of modern day "white-trash."

Flat chat, flat out - Moving as fast as possible; hence, busy.

Flick - To "give (something or somebody) the flick" is to get rid of it or him/her.

Flog - To sell something or to steal something or to treat something roughly.

Fly wire - Gauze flyscreen covering a window or doorway.

Footpath - Any well-used walkway.

Fossick - To prospect, for example for gold; hence to search, to rummage.

Franger – Condom.

Fremantle doctor - The cooling afternoon breeze that arrives in Perth from the direction of Freeo.

Fuck truck - A panel van fitted out with mattress in the back for amorous liaisons.

Fugly - Fucking ugly.

Furphy - False or unreliable rumour.

G

Garn - Go on; going; for example "Garn y'mongrel."; see carn.

Ganda or gander - To take a look at something.

G'day - Dood day, hello.

Give it a burl - Try it, have a go.

Gobful, give a - To abuse, usually justifiably.

Gobsmacked - Surprised, astounded.

Going off - Used of a night spot or party that is a lot of fun.

Good oil - Useful information, a good idea, the truth.

Good onya - Good for you, well done.

Goon - Cheap cask wine.

Gun - Of excellent ability.

H

Hang shit - To mock, sully, denigrate, slander; to "pay out."

Hills Hoist - A type of rotary clothes-line.

Heaps - A lot; very. To "give someone heaps" is to pour mockery and/or abuse on them.

Heaps good- South Australian term to mean "very good".

Hooly dooley - A term used when something out of the ordinary happens.

Hoon - To drive fast, loudly, and irresponsibly.

Hooroo – Goodbye.

Hottie - Hot water bottle.

How ya gahn - How have you been/how are you doing.

Humpy - Small Aboriginal shelter, or any temporary outdoor shelter.

I

Idiot box - A television set.

J

Jet - To go somewhere in a hurry.

Jaded - Feeling hungover or suffering the after effects of drugs.

K

Kangaroos loose in the top paddock - Intellectually inadequate.

Kenoath - Contraction of "fucking oath."

Kero – Kerosene.

Kick on - Partying on after a discotheque or night club has finished.

Kindie – Kindergarten.

Knackered - Tired, exhausted.

Knock - To criticise

Knock back - (noun) Refusal, (transitive verb) Refuse

Knock up - Make pregnant (from the U.S.) or wake up in the morning (from the U.K.) or hit on the side (or back) of the head

L

Lend of, to have a - To take advantage of somebody's gullibility.

Light globe - An incandescent light bulb.

Lingo - Language or dialect.

Lippy – Lipstick.

Lob or lob in - Drop in to see someone.

London to a brick - Absolute certainty for example "It's London to a brick that taxes won't go down."

Long paddock - The side of the road where livestock is grazed during droughts.

Lunch box, open one's - To fart.

Lurk - Illegal or underhanded racket.

M

Manchester - Household linen.

Mangkin - A common, often Western Australian expression used to describe the behaviour of someone on drugs.

Mate's rate or mate's discount - Cheaper than usual for a friend.

Matilda - Swagman's bedding, sleeping roll.

Metho - Methylated spirits.

Mickey Mouse - Excellent, very good; inconsequential.

Milk bar - A shop where milk-shakes and other refreshments can be bought.

Moll - Used to describe a person or persons who have perpetrated an act, spoken words, or generally just 'done something' to annoy the user of this word.

Mozz or to put the mozz on – Jinx.

Mungin' - To eat veraciously; to perform oral sex.

Munted - Either broken, mangled or state of inebriation.

Muntyhead - One who likes to get munted.

Muster - Round up sheep or cattle.

N

Nah - No. "nah, im too busy."

Natio – Nationality.

Nasho - National Service (compulsory military service).

Nature strip (or verge in Western Australia) - A lawn or plantation in the road reserve between the property boundary and the street.

No drama - Same as no worries.

No sweat - Same as no worries.

No worries or nurries - You're welcome; no problem.

Nong (or ning-nong) - An idiot.

Noon - As opposed to the British English midday.

Norgs – Breasts.

Not the full quid - Not bright intellectually.

No wuckin' furries - A spoonerism of no fuckin' worries, has the same usage as no worries.

Nut out - Hammer out; work out.

O

Occy strap - Elastic strap with hooks on the ends for securing items.

Okey-dokey – OK.

On ya bike - As in "get on your bike."

Onya - A congratulatory term.

Op shop - Opportunity shop, thrift store, place where second hand goods are sold.

P

Paddock - See 'long paddock.'

Paro/parro – Drunk.

Pearler - An excellent example of something.

Perv - Short for pervert.

Pez - Something of poor value or perceived to be less worthy than others.

Piece of piss - Easy task.

Pig's arse - I don't agree with you.

Pinged - Caught doing something wrong.

Pink slip, get the - Get fired.

Piss – Beer.

Pissed – Drunk.

Pissed off - Angry.

Pissing into the wind - Futile efforts.

Piss in the woods - Simple, easy.

Piss-fart around - To waste time.

Piss off - To get lost; to leave.

Piss-weak or piss-poor - Weak; ineffectual; pathetic; unfair: a general purpose negative.

Pissing down - Raining heavy.

Pissing myself laughing - To be greatly amused. figurative.

Pokies - Poker machines, fruit machines, gambling slot machines.

Poof, poofter – Homosexual, derog.

Poofteenth - A minuscule amount, a smidgen.

Porcelain bus, driving the – Vomiting into a toilet.

Porker - A lie, "he's tellin porkers" or "its just porkers."

Port - Any form of hand luggage.

Pov or povo - Cheap looking; from poverty.

Pozzy – Position.

Preggers, preggo – pregnant.

Prezzy - Present, gift.

Q

Quack - A doctor. "I have to visit the quack."

Quid, make a - Earn a living.

Quid, not the full - Of low IQ; quid is slang for a pound, £1 became $2 when Australia converted to decimal currency.

R

Rack off - Push off! get lost! get out of here! also "rack off hairy legs!".

Rage – Party.

Rage on - To continue partying - "we raged on until 3am."

Rapt - Pleased, delighted.

Ratshit - Broken, not working properly; extremely drunk.

Reckon - You bet, absolutely or giving your opinion.

Rego - Vehicle registration.

Ridgy-didge - Original, genuine.

Righto - Okay or that's right. Can also be said as rightio.

Right, that'd be - Accepting bad news as inevitable.

Rip snorter - Great, fantastic, excellent.

Ripper - Something that is excellent, great, fantastic; similar to beauty.

Rock up - To turn up, to arrive.

Root - Slang term for sex.

Ropeable - Very angry.

Rort - Cheating, fiddling, defrauding.

Rough as guts - Rough, bumpy, of poor quality.

Rubbish - To criticise.

S

Satched - To be extremely wet.

Scab - To take something with no direct recompense.

Scrag - An unattractive woman.

Scrag fight - A fight between two women, usually physical.

Scratchy - Instant lottery ticket.

Sealed road - A road covered in bitumen.

Servo - Service station (i.e. petrol station / gas station).

Sheila - Woman.

She'll be right - It will be okay.

Sheltershed, lunch shed, weather shed or undercover area - In most States a simple detached building for the protection of school children from hostile weather.

Sherbet - Beer. As in "going to to the pub for a couple of sherbets."

Shirty - Polite version of shitty or pissed off.

Shitfaced - Inebriated.

Shit-hot - Exclamation, excellent.

Shout - To treat someone or to pay for something, especially a round of drinks.

Showbag - Full of shit.

Shower in a can – Deodorant.

Shonky - Poorly made, of low quality; dishonest, dubious, underhanded.

Shoot through - To leave.

Shot - Abandoning some venture one has become sick of.

Shotgun - Derivative of 'bags', used to claim ownership.

Sick - Very good.

Sickie - A day of absence from work, sometimes due to feigned illness.

Skite - Boast, brag.

Slapper - Easy or loose female.

Slaughtered - Either extremely tired or drunk.

Sledge - To insult members of the opposing team in a sports match.

Sleepout - House veranda converted to a bedroom.

Slurry - A promiscuous young woman, similar to slut or skank.

Spare - Very angry or upset.

Spew – Vomit.

Spewin – Angry or disappointed.

Spiffy, pretty spiffy - Great, excellent.

Spit the dummy - Get very upset at something.

Spruik - To promote or sell something; cf. British flog.

Sprung - Caught doing something wrong.

Squiz - A look, as in "Take a squiz at the new house."

Standover - Using intimidation or threat of violence to coerce others.

Station - A big farm/grazing property.

Steak - A story irrelevant to the current line of conversation.

Stella - Good, pleasing, thanks.

Sticking out like dog's balls - Very obvious.

Stickybeak - To nose around.

Stoked - Very pleased.

Strewth! - Exclamation, mild oath.

Strike! - Exclamation.

Stuffed - Exhausted, tired.

Stuffed, I'll be - Expression of surprise.

Stung - Hung over; disappointed.

Sunbake – Sunbathe.

Super - Short for superannuation, the Australian term for a private retirement pension, equates to the US 401k.

Suss - Suspicious; suspect or to figure something out.

Swag - Soiled up bedding etc.

Sweet - Fine, good.

T

Ta - Thank you.

Take the piss - Taking fun of.

Tall poppy syndrome - The attitude taken by common people of resenting those who, due to social, political or economic reasons act egotistical and flaunt their success without humility.

Technicolour yawn, to have a - To vomit.

Tee-up - To set up (an appointment).

Tickets, to have on oneself - To have a high opinion of oneself.

Tight - Thrifty with money.

Tinny - Small aluminium boat, a can of beer.

Tinny, tin-arsed – Lucky.

Tits on a bull, as useful as - Something completely useless.

Toey - On edge, nervous, distracted; horny.

Togs – Swimming. costume, bathers

Too right - Definitely; that is correct.

Troppo, gone - To have escaped to a state of tropical madness.

True blue - Completely loyal to a person or belief.

Turps - Turpentine, alcoholic drink.

Two up - A gambling game played by flipping two coins simultaneously.

U

U-ey (chuck a U-ey, hang a U-ey) - Perform a U-turn in a vehicle.

Un-Australian - Considered to be an example of unacceptable behaviour or policy in Australia.

Unco - Clumsy, uncoordinated.

Uni – University.

Unit - Flat, apartment.

Up oneself - Have a high opinion of oneself.

Up somebody, get - To rebuke somebody.

Up the duff - Pregnant (i.e., my sheila's up the duff).

V

Veg out - Relax in front of the TV.

W

Wag - To skip school or work.

Walkabout - Meaning to take a journey of significant duration with no specific destination.

Wing - To pass, to give; to undertake a task.

What do you think this is, bush week? - Disbelieving response to some one you think is trying to con you.

Whatever you reckon - A dismissive to indicate

that a person is lying or
talking rubbish.

Whinge - Complain;
similar to crying, but
more commonly used for
adults.

Whiteant - To criticise
something to deter
somebody from buying
it.

**Wrap one's laughing
gear** - To eat something.

Wobbly - Excitable
behaviour.

Wog - Flu or trivial
illness.

Y

Yabber - Talk (a lot).
Yakka – Hard work.
Yarn - To talk.
Yeah-no/yeah-nah - Non-
committal expression
with various
applications.

A Note on Sources

Much of the information in this book was culled from our own knowledge of British English. We did countless hours of research watching British TV and writing down words and phrases. We also drew on several sources, including Wikipedia, Wiktionary and countless other freely available sources on the web. We wanted to make this dictionary as comprehensive as possible, so our lists of words are made up from multiple sources combined into one master list we developed on our own. We have also used words that we've learned while on our many travels throughout Britain.

ABOUT THE AUTHOR

Jonathan Thomas is the founder of Anglotopia.com - the website for people who love Britain. He's a passionate Anglophile who loves everything British. Jonathan and his wife Jackie travel to Britain often for both research and pleasure. His dream is to one day make his home in Dorset with his beautiful wife Jackie.

British Slang Submission Form

Instructions:

Is there a word missing from this dictionary? Then please let us know about it by filling out this form and mailing it in. We will include your contribution in the 2nd edition.

Word or Phrase: _____

Verb   Noun   Adverb   Acronym   Adjective
(Circle One) Other: _____

Definition:

_____
_____
_____
_____
_____

Mailing Instructions:

Send Entries To:

Anglotopia LLC
1101 Cumberland Dr #120
Valparaiso, IN 46383
USA

Made in the USA
Middletown, DE
13 March 2017